D0884697

THE FOUNDATIONS OF EDUCATION SERIES

The School and the Economic System

CHARLES S. BENSON
University of California, Berkeley

Series Editor
JUDSON T. SHAPLIN
Graduate Institute of Education
Washington University, St. Louis

S R A

Science Research Associates, Inc.
Chicago

Library of Congress Catalog Card Number: 66-15328

© 1966, Science Research Associates, Inc.
259 East Erie Street, Chicago, Illinois 60611
Printed in U.S.A.   All Rights Reserved.

Preface

The primary aim of the FOUNDATIONS OF EDUCATION SERIES is to apply current research and theory in the behavioral and social sciences to the study of American education. The series will provide students, teachers, school administrators, and other educators with illuminating examples of how and why sociologists, anthropologists, political scientists, economists, and social psychologists are contributing new directions and new vitality to the system and the process of education. Each book in the series is an original work by an author who in his own research, teaching, and writing has helped to bring about these exchanges between disciplines. Each book is problem-oriented and evidence-oriented, and none of the authors presume to give final answers to the issues they examine. Although most of the volumes concentrate on elementary and secondary education, many discuss relevant aspects of higher education.

The series as a whole could form the core of introductory or advanced courses in the social, philosophical, or historical foundations of education. But each volume is self-contained, and individual books will be useful in other courses in the education curriculum that analyze the American school system and the basic educational issues of our society. Since many such issues covered in the series have implications far beyond those of education, many of the books will provide supplementary reading for courses outside the department or school of education, especially in the behavioral and social sciences and in social and intellectual history. The books of the series will also serve as useful additions to professional libraries of individuals and school systems.

In *The School and the Economic System* Professor Benson does not presume that the reader has made any prior study of economics. He offers a relatively simple and straightforward description of the American economic system as a background for understanding both the contribution of the schools to the American economy and the economic problems of the schools themselves. There are discussions of income distribution, consumer decisions, production decisions, the role of the government in the economy, and other major topics in the framework of current economic thought. Where pertinent, the author illustrates by examples how economic principles can be applied to problems in the educational system.

Following this general description of the economic system, Professor Benson explains some of the specific economic issues and principles that affect the schools: the economic benefits of education, the cost of educational services, educational planning, efficiency in education, personnel problems, and the issue of local or state autonomy vs. federal control. He uses the comparative data he has gathered from other countries during his extensive travels to cast American problems and policies into world perspective.

Charles S. Benson, now professor of education at the University of California, Berkeley, is admirably qualified by training and experience to present this description of economics and its role in education. After training in economics at Princeton and Columbia universities, he received an appointment in economics at Bowdoin College, where he also did regional economic planning and analyses. Since 1955 he has devoted himself to the study of the economics of education, beginning at Harvard and continuing at Berkeley. He is the author of a widely used text on the economics of education and the editor of a related book of readings. Professor Benson has had broad experience in school finance at the federal, state, and local levels; he has conducted intensive state studies in Massachusetts, New York, and California; and he has served as a consultant to local school authorities in many parts of the country. As a part of his work and travel outside the United States he has made an intensive study of the finance of education in Great Britain.

In addition to this distinguished background, Professor Benson brings to his work some special interests and preoccupations that make this book engrossing reading. He is deeply committed to the principle of equal educational opportunity; this interest has led him to analyze incisively the existing educational inequalities, the methods of taxation, and the responsibilities of the local, state, and federal governments. He has sympathy for the plight of the disadvantaged, and he makes many proposals for the improvement of their education. And finally, his special interest in educational planning in both developed and underdeveloped countries adds to this book a perspective on planning which is indeed rare in any book on education.

JUDSON T. SHAPLIN

Contents

Introduction

Education has moved to the forefront of American public policy. There are high expectations that educational services will ameliorate some of our most fundamental domestic problems: youth unemployment, racial conflict, and the devitalization of our large cities, among others. At the same time, we recognize that the quality of these educational services will largely determine whether the country's economy remains strong and productive, and whether our society will be able to take advantage of the leisure that a healthy economy provides. Obviously the teacher must be in the spearhead of this national progress.

This book was written in the belief that to achieve these national goals, teachers must play an effective part in shaping educational policy. And if teachers are to share in the formation of this policy, they must be familiar with the functioning of our economy, where many problems that the schools face have their origin. (For example, the current rate of youth unemployment has been partly the result of techniques that have reduced the relative demand for unskilled labor.) But in addition, teachers must be able to carry on at least a basic dialogue with economists, who now serve important roles as advisers to legislative bodies and departments where educational policies are devised and administered. The federal government has been steadily increasing the extent of its influence over the financing and functioning of educational services. This national policy has been an uneasy compromise between our economic objectives and our economic constraints. Indeed, it might not be too great an exaggeration to say that even though the details of our national policies are established through political compromise, their general nature is determined by economic realities.

In this short volume the reader will find two discussions. The first is a description of the analytical concepts that economists use in their work. Economists are not content simply to describe industries or count job vacancies or measure the rate of inflation. They are much more interested in trying to find out why economic events occur — why, for example, we have an inflationary spiral at one time and not at another, or why firms in monopolistic markets and those in competitive industries adopt different policies. Some familiarity with the analytical concepts that economists use to study these phenomena is essential in understanding how economists view the world, and what they take into account (or do not take into account!) when they advise on public policy, including educational policy. Readers who have had a recent course in economic principles will probably find this section quite simple, while others may want to approach it more slowly. But the material has been presented as clearly as possible, and wherever it was found appropriate, illustrations have been included to show how these principles can be applied to educational policy.

The latter half of the book is devoted to a review of the economists' latest discoveries about the schools — for example, what it costs our society to provide schools services, and what benefits these services yield to our nation. Economists now discuss these benefits in both general and quantitative terms, and they relate educational expenditures to the rate of our national economic growth.

At the outset it is instructive to note that economists currently hold education in remarkable esteem. Like civilized men everywhere, they appreciate primarily the contribution that education makes to man's enjoyment of reading, his appreciation of art and music, his ability to communicate in the languages of other nationalities, his sense of man's history and scientific achievements, and his ability to converse with others who are educated. But they have now realized that education is also a major, if not a dominant, factor in our achievement of a high standard of living. The share of our economic growth that can be attributed to education (depending on one's point of view about its contribution to our achievements in research) varies from about a quarter to a half of the total. Education has had enormous effects on the improvement of the productivity of our population. But aside from these advantages, economists admit that education has also brought us definite social benefits: the preservation of the democratic order, the maintenance of social mobility, and the stimulation of the arts, as well as the satisfaction that the individual student (and his family, neighborhood, and employers) derives from his education. As educators and economists join forces more and more to shape educational policy, educators will become aware that economists are highly cognizant of all these contributions that education is making to our national life.

Chapter One: INCOME, WORK, AND LEISURE

THE RICH COUNTRY

The United States is a rich and productive country. To get a feeling for what this statement implies, imagine that you are on a trip around the world observing different peoples as they go about their daily lives. What impressions would you receive and what contrasts in typical modes of life would you sense?

As an American you might first be struck by the large number of children that families have in vast reaches of Asia, India, Africa, Latin America, and the Middle East. But you would see rather few old people—although you would probably overestimate the ages of the people you saw, because premature aging is a characteristic of these regions of the world. For the three-quarters of the globe that it is fashionable to describe as underdeveloped, it would be evident that fertility rates are relatively high (about 60 percent higher than in the United States) and that life expectancy is low (less than 40 years for males in India and the Congo, as compared with nearly 70 years in the United States). A second thing you might note is that large numbers of people in the underdeveloped countries show the ravages of disease on their faces and bodies.

If you did not confine your touring to the large capitals, you would realize that most people are engaged in agriculture (up to 70 percent of the population in many countries); moreover, men, women, and children would be working side by side in the fields. The farmers would be using agricultural tools, but these would be of a simple hand type. Sources of power would be human and animal muscle. One thing you would miss, being an American, would be evidence that these people were able to put large amounts of food aside to protect themselves against famine in case of crop failure—you would not see the huge grain silos that are so profusely scattered over our midwestern states.

The towns and villages would consist of small houses, hardly above the level of what we would call shacks, and there would be the barest minimum of public services such as paved streets, sanitation facilities, and electricity. Inside the houses you would see that the amount of furnishings, clothing, and utensils was hardly more than the families could carry on their backs if the need arose. For transportation, the people would move on foot or, if the family was relatively well off, on a bicycle, or possibly on a very crowded public bus. You would see only a few people reading anything—because about half of them are illiterate, for one thing, and because the supply of paper is quite limited, for another. There might be radio and television, but a village of five hundred souls would be proud to have one set. These are some features of life for that half of the world's population whose annual income per person is only $100.[1]

As you passed through the familiar terrain of America, what features of our life would stand out in contrast to what you had just observed in the underdeveloped nations? The age distribution of the population would be different, of course: fewer babies and more old people. The people would appear to be physically larger and healthier than those in other parts of the world. You would see that the work force was engaged in an enormous variety of tasks, with relatively few people working in agriculture and the extractive industries (mining, for example) and relatively many in the service fields, such as transportation, communication, finance, and education. Indeed, you might well wonder how such a vastly complex set of economic activities can be coordinated so that the right goods and services get to the right place at the right time. You would see that Americans appear to desire a large amount of living space; they like to raise their families in detached houses, each with a bit of ground around it. But perhaps the chief single feature of our life that you would find in startling contrast to that of the underdeveloped nations is the great amount of physical capital we use: steel mills; oil refineries; giant computers; huge

---

[1]For a discussion of international differences in income, see Everett E. Hagen, "Some Facts About Income Levels and Economic Growth," *Review of Economics and Statistics*, February 1960.

earthmoving machines; agricultural machines to till the ground, plant the seed, and harvest the crops; automobiles and airplanes — not to forget the $1000 worth of capital goods (refrigerators, washers, etc.) that the typical housewife uses to carry out her duties.[2] (Capital goods, defined here as including automobiles and household appliances, have a finite life: the old ones are discarded and replaced. And therefore, perhaps the ultimate symbol of the distinction between American affluence and the poverty of the majority of the people in the world is the dump or junkyard, which is ubiquitous in our landscape.)

The other type of capital that we possess and use, the stock of educated people in our society, might not be apparent to you from your travels. Through the combined use of intellectual and physical capital, Americans have obtained a high degree of control over their environment: the courses of rivers are changed to irrigate the deserts and make them fertile; food is raised and stored in such plenty that no one fears famine; disease is reduced in incidence and severity; and while the weather is not yet subject to our control in any significant degree, it is no great difficulty for us to protect ourselves from the discomfort of heat and cold. Thus are the ancient scourges of mankind exorcised, while at the same time we have perfected instruments of communication and travel that would hardly have been imagined even a half century ago.[3]

Between 1930 and 1963 expenditures per person on "consumption goods" rose from $976 to $1746, even after an adjustment is made for changes in prices, that is, "inflation." To gain a notion of what these particular figures mean, the reader is requested to make another imaginary journey, a journey backward in time to 1930 to consider what the patterns of consumption were in that day.

To begin with the food category, quick-frozen foods in all their variety did not exist, and people in general ate fewer fresh green vegetables but more starchy food, such as bread, potatoes, and rice. For most families it was a very special occasion to have a meal in a restaurant. Clothing differed in style, of course, but winter clothing was also heavier than we are now accustomed to, because car heaters were not in common use and home heat often was not thermostatically controlled. People lived either on farms or rather close to the centers of cities, and they made much more use than we do of urban transportation, particularly the electric streetcar. Houses had rather small rooms and no large expanses of glass in the walls. Housewives lacked the conveniences of automatic washers, driers, and disposals. Commercial television did not

---

[2] One measure of our affluence is that household capital goods are allowed to stand idle for many hours of the working week.

[3] It is also worth noting that income per person in the United States is approximately twice as high as it is in some of the culturally advanced nations of Western Europe, such as France, the United Kingdom, and Norway.

exist, nor did direct-dial telephoning. Indeed, even the radio and electric phonograph were still novelties. Life and other photo-newsmagazines had not yet appeared, and paperbound books were not generally available. Sailing, skiing, and golf remained sports for rich households, not for those of moderate means. The scientific basis for modern medicine had been established, but diseases such as pneumonia, tuberculosis, and infantile paralysis killed and crippled people in numbers that we would regard as horrendous today. Families did not participate in federal social security programs; this meant that they faced a rather grim economic future when the principal wage earner died or retired. Unemployment compensation programs had not yet been established on a sound fiscal basis, so the specter of deprivation and the actual indignity of standing in bread lines were features of life never far removed from people's consciousness.

To illustrate the change in consumption patterns even more sharply, consider the young executive who rises on a summer's morning to start another day of work. After shaving with his electric razor, he dons his wash-and-wear shirt and puts on his Dacron suit and his shoes of synthetic leather. He has a breakfast of frozen orange juice, a roll (which his wife has just taken from the freezer and popped into a wall-mounted oven), and instant coffee. He places his dirty dishes in the automatic dishwasher, kisses his wife goodbye while noting that she is still wearing her plastic hair rollers, strolls through the family room and strikes a chord on the electric organ, walks out through the aluminum-framed door, and stumbles over a glass fishing rod his son has carelessly left on the path to the carport. He climbs into his automobile, turns on the air conditioning, and drives to work listening to the morning news on his transistorized radio. Now, all the things mentioned in this paragraph are new consumer goods. They have all been placed on the market since 1930, and most of them much later than that, except for the house, the car, and the dirty dishes.

Between 1930 and 1964 the share of consumption expenditures for food declined from 27.4 to 23 percent. This occurred despite the fact that expenditures on restaurant meals and beverages increased by about 580 percent (compared with an overall rise in consumption expenditures of 463 percent) and in spite of the fact that the food housewives purchase in stores is much more highly processed now than it was in 1930. Similarly, the shares of consumption expenditures for housing and clothing have declined. On the other hand, expenditures on medical services, transportation, books and magazines, education, and foreign travel have risen at noticeably higher rates than the average of all expenditures.[4]

---

[4]U.S. Department of Commerce, National Income, 1954 edition, pp. 206–8, and Survey of Current Business, July 1965, p. S-1 (Washington: Government Printing Office.) In this instance the figures are uncorrected for price change; they are estimated in "current dollars."

Thus the United States, which is already rich by world standards, is increasing the volume and changing the character of its consumption expenditures. Though one may have reservations about certain aspects of modern American life—the blight of our central cities, perhaps, or the facelessness of life in the suburbs, or the triviality in the commercial arts—it is fair to say that most people find it more agreeable to live in an expanding economy than in a stagnant or declining one; to live, that is, with the expectation that one's income will be at least as high in the future as it is now (and perhaps a little higher), rather than to face with one's neighbors the prospect of ever more austerity ahead. And this takes us right to the central topics of economics. The economist is always seeking better answers to these two closely related questions: (1) What are the sources of economic growth? (2) What set of policy measures is most likely to promote a high rate of growth? It should be noted that in recent years a group of economists has come to the view that a large share of past economic growth is explained (or accounted for) by the rising volume of educational expenditures: this a matter to which we will give considerable attention in Chapters 6–8.

MORE LEISURE AS WELL

In the course of its history the United States has accumulated vast quantities of physical and intellectual capital. These stocks of capital have increased our productivity, and as we have just noted, this rise in productivity has allowed us to consume many more goods and services than we did in earlier years. But part of our growing capacity to produce has been expended in the form of greater amounts of leisure time. In 1900 the prevailing workweek in manufacturing was 59.5 hours, and paid vacations were practically unknown. In 1963 the average hours per week were 40.0, and the typical employee could expect to receive two weeks of paid vacation. A conservative estimate for 1980 is a workweek of 37.5 hours and an average of three weeks of paid vacation.[5] The continuing decline of hours worked is in itself a factor that increases the demand for educational services, because there are "educational prerequisites" for leisure as well as, of course, for work.

THE NEW STRUCTURE OF WORK

For untold centuries "work" for most people meant the use of their muscles to plant, till, and harvest crops and to move and fabricate objects,

---

[5]John W. Kendrick, *Productivity Trends in the United States* (Princeton, N.J.: Princeton Univ. Press, 1961), p. 445; and Edward F. Denison, *The Sources of Economic Growth in the United States and the Alternatives Before Us* (New York: Committee for Economic Development, 1962), p. 37.

with or without partial assistance from "machines." In America and the industrialized world generally, human brainpower has taken the place of the large muscles as the instrument of work, and now, indeed, machines even perform those computations and make those decisions that can be described to them in a straightforward, logical way. Thus machines have been assigned the performance of most physical work, and they are now employed in tasks that formerly required the exercise of considerable human brainpower.

The expanding role of the machine has somewhat predictable effects on the occupational structure of the labor force. Fig. 1 indicates the change in the number of persons in different occupations between 1950 and 1960, and the changes that are expected to take place by 1975. In spite of the fact that the number of employed persons is expected to rise by 28 million between 1950 and 1965, the number of "operatives" (semiskilled, nonclerical employees) is forecast to rise by only 2.1 million. It is estimated that unskilled workers will stay approximately constant in number with only a slight rise of 200,000, while the number of farmers and farmworkers will fall by 3.5 million. What, then, will the large number of new workers do? They will engage mainly in professional activities, in white-collar work, and in the highly skilled mechanical trades. For example, the employment category of professional and technical workers is forecast to expand by 7.9 million persons, an increase of 175 percent. The number of clerical workers is expected to increase by 6.6 million, which represents an approximate doubling of their number. The number of craftsmen and foremen is forecast to increase by 3.5 million (a rise of 45 percent).

These changes in the occupational structure reflect the interplay of several characteristics of our growing economy. For one thing, as a society becomes richer, the people in it are likely to consume relatively fewer goods, such as food, clothing, and housing, and relatively more services, such as medical care, transportation, and cultural-recreational programs. We noted this tendency in our discussion of the changing pattern of consumption. Another change in our occupational structure is due to the advance in productivity (output per worker), which has been phenomenal in the manufacturing, mining, and agricultural fields, but not so great in the service fields generally. For example, in electronic plants it is now possible for two men using automated equipment to assemble a thousand radios a day, whereas two hundred men would have been required to do the same work in 1950.[6] The time to make an automobile engine block has been reduced from 24 hours to 14.6 minutes. Similar dramatic advances have occurred in agriculture and the extractive industries. Naturally, then, fewer people are needed to produce goods in these fields.

---

[6]Gerald G. Somers, Edward L. Cushman, and Nat Weinberg (eds.), *Adjusting to Technological Change* (New York: Harper & Row, 1963), pp. 13-15.

FIG. 1

EMPLOYMENT BY MAJOR OCCUPATIONAL GROUPS 1950-1975

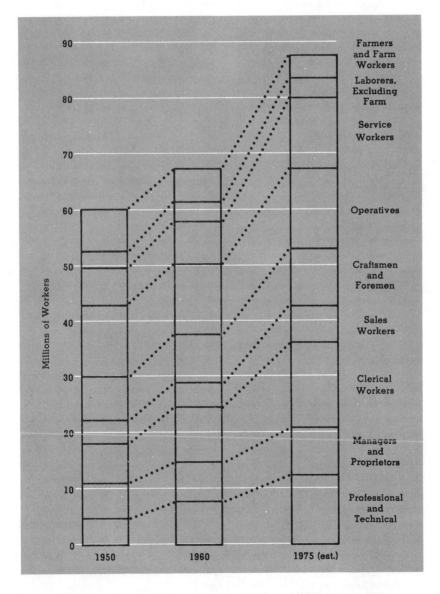

Source: U.S. Department of Labor, Report on Manpower Requirements, Resources, Utilization, and Training, 1964, pp. 199, 244.

Also, jobs themselves change. The "production workers" of the future will typically be machine monitors. "They may have responsibility for supervising complexes of automatic equipment (sometimes a battery of machines), for controlling an integrated system of conveyors and processing machines from a remote station, or for monitoring an elaborate instrument control panel and recording information for interpretation."[7] Whether such workers should be classified as operatives, technicians, or clerks is not yet clear. At the higher professional levels in science and engineering, the demand for "imaginative and resourceful people appears to be without limit, and specialization is proceeding apace. Such fields as cryogenics, bionics, ultrasonics, computer technology, and microelectronics were little known a decade ago."[8] Finally, there has been a substantial expansion of employment in government, which we shall discuss in Chapter 4. Public employment is heavily concentrated in the professional fields (science, teaching, etc.) and the clerical fields. These are some of the factors that undergird the shift in the occupational structure in our society.

Changes in technology and the associated shifts in the occupational distribution of the labor force raise several questions about education. (1) To what extent is the "technological revolution" a consequence of the past investments that the United States has made in the schooling of its people? (2) What changes in vocational education, broadly defined, are sensible in the light of the continuing shift toward white-collar employment? (3) Is it feasible for education, as an industry in its own right, to share in the technological advances that are now characteristic of most sectors of our economy — that is, can there be a dramatic rise in the efficiency of the schools' services? These are questions to which we will return again and again in this book.

SOME PROBLEMS REMAIN

Throughout its history the discipline of economics has been concerned with social problems. At various times American economists have concentrated their attention on problems of monopoly power, the supply of money and international liquidity, and the tax system. In the 1930s the overriding area of interest was in halting the worldwide depression and establishing a set of international and domestic programs which would make the repetition of such economic catastrophes unlikely. In the 1950s economists concentrated their thoughts on combating inflation in the domestic economy and on im-

---

[7]U.S. Department of Labor, *Manpower Report of the President and A Report on Manpower Requirements, Resources, Utilization, and Training* (Washington: Government Printing Office, 1964), p. 61.

[8]*Ibid.*, p. 62.

proving living standards in the underdeveloped regions of the world. All these problems, and others of long-standing interest, continue to occupy the attention of some economists, but presently the two closely related dominant domestic issues appear to be (1) the lagging rate of economic growth and (2) the failure of some groups in our own country to share in the progress we are making. Since we have been discussing the great wealth of the United States and the changing patterns of consumption and work (work which is at once more intellectually demanding and less physically arduous), and since we have also spoken of the associated blessings of longer life, better health, and greater leisure, it may seem strange that these present problems stress the lack of economic advance for the country and especially for certain groups within it; but this is the case.

1. *The Lagging Growth Rate.* If one added up the value of all goods and services produced in the various countries of the world, one would find that certain nations, notably France, Germany, Japan, and the U.S.S.R., have on the average an annual increase in this value of from 5 to 8 percent a year. Aside from such stimulating crises as the Vietnamese war, the rate of growth in national product in the United States in recent years has been only about 3 percent a year. Some of the difference between ourselves and other advanced nations in this respect is understandable. Because the United States is one of the richest countries, it is experiencing one of the largest shifts of economic activity from the goods to the service sector of the economy, and the service sector cannot be expected to show as rapid gains in production as the goods sector. Nonetheless, it is a matter of concern that our growth rate appears low relative to that of other countries, particularly when one considers that the United States has a relatively high rate of "involuntary leisure," or unemployment.

2. *The Disadvantaged Groups.* From 1958 to the present time the percentage of experienced wage and salary workers who are unemployed (but able and willing to work) has averaged about 5½ percent. Among industrial countries this is a relatively high rate of unemployment. In 1960-61, for example, France, West Germany, Japan, and Sweden reported rates of less than 2 percent, while Great Britain's rate stood at the comparatively low level of 2.4 percent.[9] Now, if our unemployment rate could be reduced to the level prevailing in these other countries by "expanding the opportunities for gainful employment and adjusting the skill and geographic composition of the work force to

---

[9] R. J. Myers and J. H. Chandler, "Comparative Levels of Unemployment in Industrial Countries," in *Measuring Employment and Unemployment* (President's Committee to Appraise Employment and Unemployment Statistics; Washington: Government Printing Office, 1962), as quoted in Seymour L. Wolfbein, *Employment and Unemployment in the United States: A Study of the American Labor Force* (Chicago: Science Research Associates, 1964), p. 319.

the evolving pattern of labor demands,"[10] then our total output would rise and our growth rate might more nearly approximate the rates achieved by European countries and Japan.

But worse still, unemployment, especially long-term unemployment, is overwhelmingly concentrated among certain groups in the society. The very young and the relatively old have high unemployment rates, as do Negroes, persons with less than a high school education, and the unskilled. On the other hand, it is a rare thing for a white, second-generation college graduate working in a professional field or in an executive position to be subject to involuntary unemployment for an extended period.

Unemployment, together with the possession of low-valued or obsolete skills, keeps many American families in poverty. It is true, of course, that public services offer relatively more benefits to the poor than to the rich, and that these have been expanded greatly since World War II. It is also true that poor families today have a higher standard of living than they did in the 1930s, for example. But a significant number of families are not sharing in the abundance the economy is providing. One way to see this is by following a statistical exercise. First, rank all households in the country by the income they receive in a year, lowest to highest. Second, divide this list into five equal parts, so that we can speak of the bottom fifth of households ranked by income, the second fifth, and so on to the top fifth. Third, find out what share of total income the bottom 20 percent of households receive and how this percentage has changed over time. Here is the answer: In 1935 the bottom fifth of households ranked by income received 4 percent of the total income in the country; in 1961 they received 5 percent of the total income — a gain of 1 percentage point in a quarter of a century! Fig. 2 shows the share received by all quintiles in these two years.

Another glimpse of the inequities in our national prosperity can be had by examining statistics on income per person in different states of the Union. The figures below show that income per person is twice as high in our richest states as it is in the poorest. Such a discrepancy makes it difficult for the poor states to provide a high quality of education, which is exactly what they need to do in order to make economic advances.

---

[10]N. J. Simler, "The Structural Hypothesis and Public Policy," *American Economic Review*, December 1964, p. 1000. Of course, unemployment can also be reduced by compulsory retirement programs, shortening of work weeks, and the like. These are devices to reduce the potential output of the economy to its actual level. What the quotation from Simler implies is that the United States might choose policies to raise the actual output to its potential.

FIG. 2
SHARES OF NATIONAL INCOME RECEIVED BY QUINTILES
OF HOUSEHOLDS, RANKED BY INCOME, 1935 AND 1962

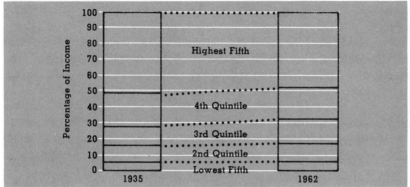

Source: U.S. Department of Commerce, *Historical Statistics of the United States,*
1789-1945, p. 15; *Survey of Current Business*, April 1964, p. 8.

Personal Income per Person: Five Rich and Five Poor States, 1964

United States Average	$2566
Rich States	
Delaware	3460
Connecticut	3281
Nevada	3248
New York	3162
California	3103
Poor States	
Kentucky	1830
Alabama	1749
Arkansas	1655
South Carolina	1655
Mississippi	1438

SOURCE: U.S. Department of Commerce, *Survey of Current Business*,
July 1965, p. 11.

These are some of our current economic problems. Policies are now being
devised and implemented to attack them, and as all readers of this book know,
educational policy is being shaped to assist in the endeavor. The forced-draft
kind of prosperity that war brings — even a small war like Vietnam — may
obscure the fact that these are abiding economic problems, but they are such,
nevertheless.

A NOTE ON INCOME MEASUREMENT

At various times we shall make reference to *income* of the nation, of the states, of households, etc., so we should have a notion of what the measurements mean. Figures on household income, whether collected by the Bureau of the Census or such groups as the Survey Research Center of the University of Michigan, refer to cash income, except personal gifts, received by the household during the stated year. The figures correspond to the gross income reported by a taxpayer on his federal income tax return, and basically they are obtained in the same way, that is, by asking the head of the household to recall what his cash income for the year was.

However, when one sees references to gross national product, national income, or the income of some particular state, one is looking at estimates prepared by the national income statisticians of the U.S. Department of Commerce. The national income statistician seeks a measure which is in some respects narrower and in some respects broader than the type of household income measure we mentioned just above; and the reason is that he is seeking figures which will accurately reflect changes in the economy's performance. He has developed his art to a high degree, and there are actually a whole set of national income measurements. Each is rather complex, but the following brief descriptions should be adequate for the present needs of the reader.

1. *Gross National Product.* This figure is the largest of the series in magnitude. It is an estimate of the total of the market value of all "final" goods and services produced in the country during a year (or quarter of a year). The word *final* is the important one, because the statistician does not wish to include the value of the loaf of bread on the grocer's shelf and the value of the flour, milk, and other ingredients that went into making the bread. This would be double counting, and one avoids double counting by measuring the market value of goods at their point of final sale (the point of final sale of the bread is the supermarket, let us say). Also, note that to be counted, the article must be newly produced in the current year. What is counted is not the value of secondhand cars that are sold, but only the value of the services, such as holding inventories, that are provided to the public by secondhand car dealers. The major components of GNP are consumption goods and services, investment goods (new machines, factories, etc.), and government services.

2. *Net National Product.* In manufacturing the gross national product for any year, some machinery and other capital goods are worn out and must be replaced. A part of the investment goods component of GNP, therefore, represents replacement of these worn-out items and does not stand for any addition to productive capacity — it is necessary just for maintaining the present economic position. To take care of this problem, the statisticians prepare an estimate of the depreciation in capital goods that has occurred in

the current period. The figure for depreciation is subtracted from GNP to obtain NNP, which conceptually is the soundest measure of our economic growth.

3. *National Income.* An estimate of indirect business taxes is subtracted from NNP to obtain the national income. National income is the sum of wages, salaries, rent, interest, and profits of the people in the country — in other words, "factor income." Now, how can we be sure that an estimate of production of goods and services, after a few adjustments (such as subtracting depreciation and business taxes) have been made, represents the income people receive? The statistician might reply airily, "Well, people don't receive income unless they produce something and people don't produce anything without getting paid for it." However, it may be more understandable if we use the concept of "value added." Consider the progress of $100 worth of bread, retail value, through its stages of production. We begin with a self-sufficient farmer who grows wheat and sells $20 worth to a flour mill. The flour mill purchases the wheat, and its cost for intermediate materials is $20. The mill then sells flour to a bakery for $50. Now, the mill has "added a value" of $30 ($50 in sales minus $20 for materials and supplies bought from other firms) to the product at this stage. The remainder of the transaction can be shown in tabular form. Note that the sum of the values added at all stages of production, $100, is equal to the market value of the bread at the point of final sale, $100. But what does the added value consist of? It consists of wages and salaries of employees at the various stages of manufacture, of rent, interest, and profit.

Stage of Production	Sales Receipts	Purchase from Other Firms	Value Added
Farmer	$20	$00	$20
Miller	50	20	30
Bakery	80	50	30
Retailer	100	80	20
		Total	$100

In short, it consists of factor income. Thus the final value of goods and services has the same value, approximately, as factor income; or, to put it another way, income and product are two sides of the same coin.

4. *Personal Income.* The national income statistician is also interested in how much money the households as a group have to spend. He therefore adjusts national income estimates by subtracting such things as profit earned by corporations but not distributed in the current period, and by adding such things as government transfer payments (veterans' benefits, for example), to obtain a measure called personal income. Private transfers like the $100 your rich aunt gives you for your birthday are still not included.

5. *Disposable Income.* This is personal income with direct federal taxes, such as the personal income tax, deducted. It is the truest measure provided by the national income statisticians of the money that households can use for consumption or put aside as savings.

The figures below show the magnitude of national income estimates for the United States.

Dollar Magnitude of Estimates of National Product and Income, 1964

	(billions)
Gross national product	$622.6
Net national product	569.1
National income	510.1
Personal income	491.4
Disposable income	431.8

SOURCE: Office of Business Economics, U.S. Department of Commerce, *Survey of Current Business*, July 1965, p. 4.

This chapter has offered some observations on the accomplishments and problems of our economic system. The next four chapters will deal with how the system works.

Suggested Readings

BAUER, PETER T., and YARNEY, BASIL S. *The Economics of Underdeveloped Countries.* Chicago: Univ. of Chicago Press, 1957.

HEILBRONER, ROBERT I . *The Great Ascent: The Struggle for Economic Development in Our Time.* New York: Harper & Row, 1963.

LEIBENSTEIN, HARVEY. *Economic Backwardness and Economic Growth.* New York: Wiley, 1957.

MILLER, HERMAN P. *Rich Man, Poor Man.* New York: Thomas Y. Crowell, 1964.

RUGGLES, RICHARD and NANCY D. *National Income Accounts and Income Analysis.* 2d ed. New York: McGraw-Hill, 1956.

United States Department of Labor. *Manpower Report of the President and A Report on Manpower Requirements, Resources, Utilization, and Training.* Washington: Government Printing Office, 1965.

Chapter Two: THE CONSUMER AND HIS DECISIONS

THE PRIMACY OF CONSUMPTION

It has already been suggested that we have a complex economic system. Our work force of 79,000,000 persons engage in 22,000 different types of occupations. Approximately 8,500,000 of these persons are self-employed; most of the rest work for about 4,800,000 private companies (4,485,000 establishments in retail, wholesale, and service fields and 315,000 in the manufacturing area) and for 92,000 units of government (local, state, and federal). The number of individual services provided and the number of final and intermediate goods produced in any given month are incalculable. Even your friendly neighborhood druggist stocks about 24,000 different items. Every day millions of decisions are made about what things (and how many of each) are to be produced, about how to produce them, and about where to deliver them. Conceivably, some central economic agency, armed with computers and all the gadgetry of modern electronic data processing, could make these decisions — or at least it could make judgments about allocations of resources

to broad areas of economic activity — but in the United States we have pre-
ferred to retain a rather extreme form of decentralization in economic decision making.[1]

On the face of it, our decentralized economic system appears to be working
well. Americans take justifiable pride in their standard of living. Consumers
ordinarily express pleasure about the new cars and new houses they buy. There
are no widespread complaints about the quality of food and clothing they
consume. Significantly, Americans are not accustomed to "queuing up" to
obtain some article or other in a store; we do not find it necessary to ration
goods on the "first-come, first-served" basis. However, to judge the performance of an economy on the basis of consumers' satisfactions is to suggest
something very important about our society, namely, that the satisfaction of
consumers' preferences is an ultimate goal of economic activity; "directly and
indirectly, most of the work done in an economy has its ultimate payoff and
purpose in the realm of consumption."[2] In the United States we take it as an
article of faith, moreover, that the individual household, not the central
government, is the best judge of what it wishes to consume.

If consumers' preferences are to direct the activities of our economy, it is
necessary that there be some means of communication between the households
of the land and the business firms and governments which provide us with
goods and services. Communication is established on the one hand in the
marketplace, where through buying or refusing to buy particular commodities
at stated prices the consumer indicates to business firms which goods it will
be profitable for them to supply. In the marketplace the consumer is "voting"
with the dollars at his command, and occasionally an "election" has a dramatic
outcome. You may recall that a few years ago the Ford Motor Company, after
spending a great deal of money on product development and advertising,
launched a new car, which was called the Edsel. Consumers did not choose to
buy the Edsel in large quantities, and its production was discontinued about
two years after it was introduced. During that same time, however, people
were buying large numbers of small foreign cars, and this "vote" led eventually
to the successful introduction in America of the compact car.

The consumer votes for government services in the polling booth. The
connection between voting and the supply of public services can be seen most
clearly in local government, where voters are asked periodically to approve a
tax rate in excess of statutory maximum (in order, probably, that teachers may

---

[1]The Communist countries, in contrast, prefer to rely on a fairly high degree of
central government control of economic activities, as do some nations on the western
side of the iron curtain, notable France and the Scandinavian countries.

[2]Robert Dorfman, *The Price System* (Englewood Cliffs, N.J.: Prentice-Hall,
1964), p. 44.

receive a raise). Or they may be asked to approve a bond issue to finance the construction of new schools.

Ultimately, communication between households and the suppliers of goods and services is established by voting. The households vote either with dollars of income or votes in the polling place, depending on whether the supplier is a private firm or a public agency.

It should not be inferred that households make their choices about which goods to purchase in isolation from the society in which they live. It is reasonable to say (and a certain amount of evidence supports the claim) that the consumption pattern of a family is influenced by the purchases made by its neighbors or friends. If my neighbor buys a color TV, I might become interested in having one; if he does not, I may not give the article any amount of serious consideration. This relation has been called the "demonstration effect."[3] In addition, both private firms and public agencies seek to persuade the consumer to demand more of their products. In the private sector such persuasion takes the form of changes in product design and of advertising.[4] When local school administrators, teachers, and PTA members seek to marshal votes for a bond election, a similar process of persuasion is taking place in the public sector.

THE MECHANISM OF CHOICE

To admit that households are subject to external influences is not to say that neighbors, the advertising industry, or government dictate how people spend their money. A strong measure of independent choice remains, and it is now our task to see how — in the economists' view — these all-important decisions are made. The argument begins with three assumptions. (1) Households are not able to satisfy all their desires for goods and services; accordingly, a condition of scarcity exists and choices must be made among competing uses for the limited amount of funds (income) available. (2) Households make

---

[3]James S. Duesenberry, Income, Saving and the Theory of Consumer Behavior (Cambridge, Mass.: Harvard Univ. Press, 1949), pp. 28-32. I have suggested elsewhere that insofar as school districts can be regarded as extended households, allocating their revenues among various items of school provision, the demonstration effect applies to them as well as to private households. The choices made in District A, that is, are influenced by knowledge of budgetary allocations in Districts B, C, and D, and District A's decisions influence, in turn, those of the other school authorities. See The Economics of Public Education (Boston: Houghton Mifflin, 1961), pp. 104-10.

[4]It is a matter of some dispute whether consumers are influenced markedly or only slightly by advertising. John Kenneth Galbraith (The Affluent Society; Boston: Houghton Mifflin, 1958; Ch. 11) holds that advertising does a great deal to shape and maintain demand for privately produced goods; Duesenberry (op. cit., p. 104) is inclined to the opposite view.

their choices in a rational manner. (3) Consumption of all (or most) commodities and services is subject to the law of *diminishing marginal utility*.[5]

This last assumption takes a bit of explaining. The notion is that the increment in utility or satisfaction from the consumption of one more unit of a commodity takes on a smaller and smaller value as the number of units consumed increases. If you have just drunk three glasses of milk, for example, the satisfaction you get from a fourth is less than you got from the third, and if you drink yet a fifth, it gives you less pleasure than the fourth, and so on.

Marginal utility, then, is the increment of satisfaction yielded by one additional small unit of a commodity, and we assume that marginal utility decreases as consumption of a commodity increases. Consider a household that is about to decide how to spend its week's income, and is passionately concerned about spending the income so that it purchases the maximum amount of satisfaction. How should the household allocate its money among the host of goods and services available in our economy? By following these simple steps: (1) compute the ratio of marginal utility to price for each commodity; (2) arrange its expenditure so that the values of all the ratios are equal. When these steps are followed, that is, when

$$\frac{MU_1}{Price\ 1} = \frac{MU_2}{Price\ 2} = \frac{MU_3}{Price\ 3} = \cdots = \frac{MU_n}{Price\ n},$$

then the household is in a position of equilibrium — no further switching among commodities can improve its level of satisfaction.

To illustrate the principle of equilibrium more clearly, let us suppose that every commodity has a price of $1 and let us concentrate our attention on two commodities, bread and milk. Suppose the family spends its money in the given week in such a way that the last unit of bread offers it 11 "utiles" of satisfaction and the last unit of milk offers it only 9. The family has not followed its instructions, because

$$\frac{Marginal\ utility\ (bread)}{Price\ of\ bread} = \frac{11}{\$1} \neq \frac{9}{\$1} = \frac{Marginal\ utility\ (milk)}{Price\ of\ milk}$$

---

[5]The "theory of consumer demand" can be built on a more respectable psychological basis than Assumption 3 (diminishing marginal utility) by using the concept of indifference curves. However, that technique is more complicated and the conclusions one draws from the two alternative techniques are identical. Hence we have chosen to employ the nineteenth century approach to consumer demand. A clear exposition of the newer view is given in Dorfman, *op. cit.*, Chapter 3.

The household, indeed, has made an improper choice, for had it spent $1 less on milk, it would have forgone approximately 9 utiles, but it could have used the dollar to buy an additional unit of bread, yielding approximately 11 utiles, and as a result it would have raised its level of satisfaction by approximately 2 utiles. If the family had followed its instructions and chosen the assortment of goods to make the ratios equal, obviously it could make no gain by shifting its purchases from one commodity to another.

But how can we be sure that the family can spend its income in such a way that the ratios finally become equal? This is where the principle of diminishing marginal utility comes in. In the above example, when the household reduces its expenditure on milk by $1 (equal to one unit of milk), the marginal utility of milk will rise slightly and, similarly, as it adds the $1 to its expenditure on bread, the marginal utility of bread will decline slightly, that is, it will represent a little less than 11 utiles. As this process continues, the two ratios should become equal, possibly in the neighborhood of 10 utiles per dollar for both bread and milk.

The economist does not suggest, of course, that families go around counting utiles. This does not invalidate his theory, however. As long as the three assumptions about scarcity, rationality, and diminishing marginal utility hold, families will behave approximately as the economist describes through a process of trial and error. This is our first example of "economic logic," a branch of analysis simple in its outlines but valuable in giving an understandable picture of the basis of making choices. The important thing to note is that choices are made on the basis of incremental or marginal values. One does not need to try to estimate the total satisfactions that a consumer receives or even the total he receives from some particular commodity. In fact, if the consumer approached the process of choice on the basis of trying to maximize total satisfactions for goods each taken one at a time, his household would face budgetary chaos.

Another thing to note is that the economic logic has great generality. Suppose a teacher is trying to allocate his time over a weekly period among various instructional activities. Then suppose that after he has made his preliminary allocation he finds that (by his best judgment) the last hour that he is spending on small group reading has twice as much instructional value as the last hour that he is spending on a spelling test. He would do well to shift an hour from spelling tests to small group reading and to continue shifting time until the instructional values of both spelling tests and small group reading are equal. Until they are equal, he is not making the best use of that last hour. It is just this kind of reasoning that underlies the formation of consumer choice, and it is consumer choice, in turn, that directs our elaborate and complex economic system.

ELASTICITIES AND ALL THAT

From the law of diminishing marginal utility we have an intuitive basis for postulating that the "demand curve" will "slope downward to the right." Now, what does all this mean? Suppose we take the case of a household that has arranged its purchases nicely for the week and has, moreover, kept a few dollars back for savings. Its array of purchases included, say, 10 loaves of bread that cost 30 cents each. What might have persuaded the family to buy 11 or 12 loaves instead of the 10 it actually purchased? One thing could have been a fall in the price of bread—to 25 cents, perhaps. The eleventh loaf, of course, yields less utility to the family than did the tenth, so the family needs some inducement to expand its purchases. One such inducement, then, is for the seller to offer a lower price, which, for a particular family, offsets the decline in utility.

Fig. 2a portrays this relation between the price and the quantity purchased. On the vertical axis we mark dollars and cents; this is the scale by which price is measured, and the higher up the line we go, the higher the price. The horizontal axis measures quantity of bread purchased, with the quantities becoming larger as we move to the right. The graph shows that Family A purchased 10 loaves of bread at a price of 30 cents and was willing to purchase 11 at a price of 25 cents. The line of relationship between price and quantity (demand curve) slopes downward to the right, which is to say that the quantity demanded (a) increases as the price of the commodity falls and (b) decreases as the price of the commodity rises.

PRICE ELASTICITY OF DEMAND

To describe the relation between variables the economist often makes use of the concept of elasticity. This is a handy tool to have in your mental tool box, so we will discuss the concept briefly. Consider Fig. 2b and note that the demand line for Family B is noticeably flatter (has less slope) than the line for Family A. Now, what happens in Family B when the price of bread drops by 5 cents? Family B wishes to increase its purchases a great deal. Instead of being satisfied with one extra loaf, it wants an extra four when the price goes down by a nickel. Family B's response to the fall in price is more elastic than Family A's. That is, for the given change in price Family B makes a more drastic adjustment in its purchase of bread than Family A. Of course, an adjustment is made when the price rises as well as when it falls. In the above example, suppose the initial price of bread were 25 cents. Then, as the price rose to 30 cents, Family A would reduce its consumption of bread by only one loaf, while Family B would cut back by four loaves.

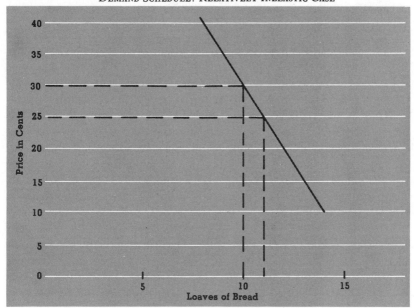

FIG. 2 a
DEMAND SCHEDULE: RELATIVELY INELASTIC CASE

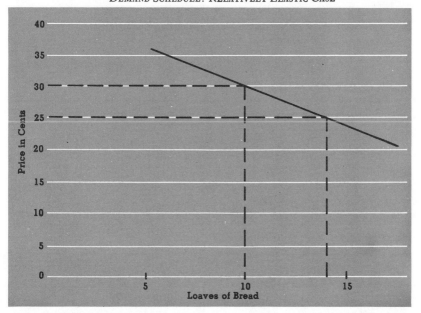

FIG. 2 b
DEMAND SCHEDULE: RELATIVELY ELASTIC CASE

Is it possible to think of a price-elastic demand for education? It is difficult in the case of public elementary and secondary education, because a workable concept of price is hard to define. However, it is clearly possible to relate fees for private schooling to the concept of price elasticity. If private secondary schools raise their fees from an average of $1200 a year to $1400, the change should have some effect on the volume of applications. If the change is quite marked, we would conclude that the demand for private education is relatively elastic; if the change is only slight, we would say that the demand is relatively inelastic. Or one could consider price elasticity in education as a factor in a bond referendum. Suppose a certain school construction program had been defeated at the polls. Subsequently there was a reduction in building costs, so that the same amount of bond money would buy a much more attractive school plant. If a second referendum were favorable to the bond issue, it would indicate in crude terms that there was a generally elastic price demand for educational services.

The slope of the demand line is roughly indicative of the price elasticity of a particular product. If the line slopes down sharply, the price is relatively inelastic; if it slopes down gently, the price is comparatively elastic. However, the economist prefers to use a somewhat more precise measure: the ratio of the percentage of change in quantity demand to the percentage of change in price. Thus,

$$\text{Price elasticity} = \frac{\text{Percentage change in quantity demanded}}{\text{Percentage change in price}}$$

For mathematical precision, the changes in price used in computing this ratio should be very small ones.

Let us use our example of how Families A and B responded to a fall in the price of bread to compute two price elasticities. For Family A we would have the following figures:

FAMILY A

Price 1	Quantity 1	Price 2	Quantity 2	Relative Change in Quantity	Relative Change in Price
30¢	10	25¢	11	1/10 = 10%	5/30 = 16.6%

Price elasticity = 10%/16.6% = .6

For Family B the results are as follows:

FAMILY B

Price 1	Quantity 1	Price 2	Quantity 2	Relative Change in Quantity	Relative Change in Price
30¢	10	25¢	14	$4/10 = 40\%$	$5/30 = 16.6\%$

Price elasticity $= 40\%/16.6\% = 2.4$

Family A's elasticity has a value less than 1, and this means, as you can readily verify, that its total expenditures on bread fall as the price of bread falls. All values of elasticity less than 1, indeed, are considered cases of "inelastic demand." Family B's elasticity has a value in excess of 1, and its expenditures on bread will rise as the price of the article falls. This is the case of elastic demand. If the value of the elasticity turns out to be precisely 1 (called the case of unitary elasticity), then total expenditures on the article remain constant as its price fluctuates. Dull things in plentiful supply, such as salt, are likely to have inelastic demand curves; pleasant things, such as strawberries, will have elastic demand schedules.

CROSS ELASTICITY OF DEMAND

A demand curve is not fixed for all time; it is expected to shift upward or downward in response to many kinds of forces. Fig. 3 shows a shift from an original curve, D_0, to a higher level of demand represented by D_1. When demand has increased, as represented by the movement from D_0 to D_1, more units of the commodity are demanded at every price. Similarly, a product can be subject to a decrease in demand, represented by the movement from D_0 to D_2. In this case less of the commodity is demanded at every price.

Demand may increase because advertisers are successful in stimulating the interest of consumers in a product. It may increase because of weather: a prolonged rainy stretch may raise the demand for umbrellas. Demand for a particular commodity may also increase (or decrease) because the price of a related product changes. A sharp rise in the price of butter may cause an increase in the demand for margarine. The two products stand in a *competitive* relation to each other, that is, they can be easily substituted for each other. On the other hand, a decline in the price of automobiles that stimulates their purchase may lead to an increase in the demand for gasoline. In this case the two products stand in a *complementary* relation to each other: consumption of one is positively associated with consumption of the other. As an exercise,

FIG. 3
SHIFTS IN DEMAND SCHEDULES

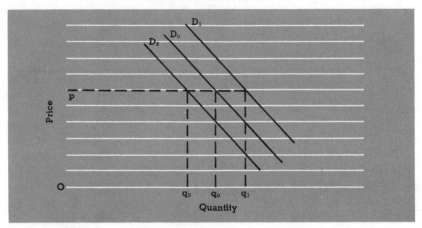

you might want to consider what goods and services are complementary to education (books and travel are obvious examples) and—this is more difficult —what goods and services are competitive with school services.[6]

The concept of cross elasticity of demand can be employed to describe the relation between competing and complementary goods:

$$\frac{\text{Cross elasticity}}{\text{of demand}} = \frac{\text{Percentage change in quantity of Commodity M demanded}}{\text{Percentage change in price of Commodity N}}$$

If the goods are complementary, the ratio will have a negative sign; if competitive, the sign will be positive.

INCOME ELASTICITY OF DEMAND

Another factor that may lead to a shift in the demand curve for a commodity is a change in the income of a household or of all the households that make up the nation. This relation is expressed as follows:

$$\text{Income elasticity of demand} = \frac{\text{Percentage change in quantity demanded}}{\text{Percentage change in income}}$$

---

[6]In a sense, all goods and services are competitive with school taxes, but the complementary-competitive principle refers to goods and services among which there is a nexus in use, so that a change in price in one of them clearly leads to a shift in the demand curve for the other.

If the ratio has a value greater than 1, the demand for the commodity increases proportionately more than the rise in income, and the opposite occurs when the income elasticity has a value less than 1. If the value is precisely 1, the amount purchased changes in exact proportion to the change in income. (For example, if income rises by 10 percentage points, the amount of the commodity purchased also rises by 10 percentage points.) Different commodities would be expected to show varying degrees of sensitivity to a change in income. A family whose income had gone up might use very little more electricity than it did before, but it might well buy a second car.

Some attempts have been made to measure the income elasticity of education. As expected, a positive relation exists, but the response of school expenditures to changes in income has not been as dramatic as one might hope. One authority found that in the United States during the years 1900-1958, a 1 percent increase in personal income per capita was associated, on the average, with a 1.09 percent increase in current expenditures on schools, per pupil in average daily attendance.[7] That is, the income elasticity of demand for public schools was represented by a value of 1.09. Another study indicated that a 1 percent increase in the proportion of families with incomes of $10,000 or more in a school district led, on the average, to an increase in per pupil expenditures of $2.74.[8] These studies were both exploratory, and it must be said that the analysis of the determinants of public school expenditures has only just begun.

A NOTE ON THE ECONOMICS OF LEISURE

The economic logic applies as well to the distribution of leisure time among various uses as it does to the distribution of a household's income among various expenditures. The rational family would allocate its time so that the last hour spent in any one pursuit yielded it the same amount of pleasure as the last hour spent in every other pursuit. In order to maximize its enjoyment, the family could trade off hours from some activity in which its interest had worn thin, for hours spent in some sport or venture in which its interest was keen.[9]

---

[7] Werner Z. Hirsch, *Analysis of the Rising Cost of Public Education*, Materials Prepared for Consideration by the Joint Economic Committee (Washington: Government Printing Office, 1959), pp. 36–37.

[8] Jesse Burkhead, *Public School Finance: Economics and Politics* (Syracuse, N.Y.: Syracuse Univ. Press, 1964), p. 69.

[9] When a household engages in some leisure activity, it ordinarily spends time and money, both of which exist in limited supply. For example, the family that takes up sailing devotes time to the activity and it also needs to find the money to buy a boat. The fact that there are "joint costs" increases the complexity of the allocation problem, though the principle of its solution remains the same.

Thus we can think of a time elasticity of demand which would show the responsiveness in a household's pursuit of particular leisure activities to an increase in the quantity of leisure it has. (As we saw in the last chapter, the amount of leisure time has notably increased in the last sixty years.) Certain activities might show a marked rise in popularity as the number of free hours increased, and these would be described as having an elastic time demand; others might not attract a significantly larger amount of attention, and these would be cases of inelastic time demand.

Education should be highly responsive to an increase of leisure. First, education can itself be regarded as a pleasurable activity; some people find enjoyment in learning something even when they expect to make no special use of the knowledge gained. Second, education is complementary to a host of other leisure activities, as any examination of "continuing education" curricula will reveal. Third, both education and its serious avocational use require the expenditure of large amounts of time. Until our society became rich enough to provide us with large amounts of leisure, many activities were too expensive in terms of time to receive serious consideration, but soon many people will give as detailed consideration to the educational preparations they make for leisure as they do to the educational preparations they make for work.

Suggested Readings

DUESENBERRY, JAMES S. Income, Saving and the Theory of Consumer Behavior. Cambridge, Mass.: Harvard Univ. Press, 1949.

FRASER, L. M. Economic Thought and Language. London: Black, 1947.

GALBRAITH, JOHN KENNETH. The Affluent Society. Boston: Houghton Mifflin, 1958.

KATONA, GEORGE; LININGER, CHARLES A.; and MUELLER, EVA. 1963 Survey of Consumer Finances. Ann Arbor: Survey Research Center, Univ. of Michigan, 1964.

SAMUELSON, PAUL A. Economics: An Introductory Analysis. 6th ed. New York: McGraw-Hill, 1964.

TINTNER, GERHARD. Mathematics and Statistics for Economists. New York: Rinehart, 1953.

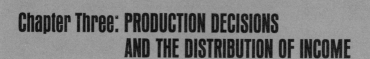

Chapter Three: PRODUCTION DECISIONS AND THE DISTRIBUTION OF INCOME

A COMPETITIVE ECONOMY

In the last chapter we discussed how households spend their income and how their spending guides the assortment of goods that is produced in our economy. Now we will discuss how it is decided what income different households receive—how it is decided, for example, that the engineer's household will have $12,000 a year to spend and the production worker's, $8000. In studying this question we shall learn something about the concept of "economic efficiency." (The concept of efficiency also has its uses in public education; it is not something that only businessmen must be concerned about.) Also, we will have another chance to apply the economic logic in solving a theoretical question.

To discuss the distribution of income, we must shift our attention from the household (or consumption) sector of the economy to the business (or production) sector.[1] The first thing to note is that our economy is competitive. Competition is the chief prod to efficiency. Any prolonged lapse into thoughtless, slovenly, or disorderly procedures by any firm is almost certain to carry economic penalties.

Attempts to avoid such penalties, however, take different forms in different types of firms. The farmer who cannot control his costs as well as the average farmer will find himself more and more deeply in debt, until finally his credit is exhausted. He will be forced to sell his farm, perhaps, or go into bankruptcy. These facts he well knows; moreover, his preoccupation with costs is realistic. The farmer cannot set his selling prices, but he can ordinarily sell all his output at whatever prices are established in the market, so when he gets into difficulties it is foolish of him to try to extricate himself by spending a lot of money on advertising, and it is equally foolish from the economic point of view for his neighbor to hold back technological advice if he has any to offer. The farmer's problems center rather exclusively on his costs per unit of output, and he is not in a state of economic rivalry with his neighbor.

Contrast this situation with the manufacture of automobiles, soap, and cigarettes. In these industries 80 percent or more of total output is produced by four or fewer firms, and industries are therefore dominated by a few giant rival enterprises. If General Motors expands its sales of automobiles by 20 percent in a single year, one can be reasonably sure that Ford and Chrysler are selling fewer cars than they did last year. Each rival seeks to persuade buyers that it offers the greatest value (for example, "the smoothest-riding, best-looking, most trouble-free, most powerful car for the dollar"). The means of persuasion are style change, product improvement, reasonable stability in price policy, and advertising. The strategies behind these means are closely held secrets in each company. If a company starts to go under, no one would expect its rivals to offer it their secrets as an ailing farmer's neighbors might.

We have given examples of two different market structures: (1) the "purely competitive" structure in which, as in agriculture, there are so many firms that no single one of them has any significant influence on prices in the selling markets (or, for that matter, in the input markets, in which labor services, land, and capital equipment are bought); and (2) the "oligopoly," in which a small number of dominant firms are rivals whose policies are dependent on the actions of the others. But in both of these market structures—and also in the other categories that the economist has devised[2]—we can

---

[1]More accurately, one might say the business-government sector, because governments produce goods and services just as business firms do. However, for reasons we shall explore later, salaries and wages are usually set in the private (or business) economy and then copied by governments.

[2]For further discussion of market structures, see Richard Caves, *American Industry: Structure, Conduct, Performance* (Englewood Cliffs, N.J.: Prentice-Hall, 1964), Chaps. 2 and 3.

properly make the assumption that the businessman seeks to maximize profits, broadly defined. By "profits broadly defined," we mean the maximum amount of money that the businessman can make without impairing his ability to make that much profit or more in later years.[3] The profit-maximizing postulate plays the same role in the theory of the business firm that the utility-maximizing postulate does in the theory of the household.

ALLOCATION DECISIONS WITHIN THE FIRM

If we assume that businessmen seek to maximize profits, we may consider how they choose between various alternative schemes of production. You might answer, "Well, of course, they would choose the particular plan of production that gives them the most return in profits." So far so good, but we are left with the question of how the businessman can tell which plan is the best at a given time. Ordinarily a commodity — a radio, say — can be produced with much material (including waste material) and little labor, or less material and more labor. The kinds of material and parts that can be put into the radio exist in bewildering array, and so do the types of machines and machine tools that can be employed. There are choices to make about what kinds of wage and salary workers to employ and how many of each; there are questions of whether or not to use part-time and overtime work arrangements. There are choices about how much and what kinds of advertising to use, and so on almost indefinitely.

The question we are dealing with is an important one in schools as well as in industrial plants. Suppose it is accepted as school policy that all children shall be brought up to a certain standard of proficiency in reading by the end of the third full year of schooling, insofar as this is humanly possible. Suppose further that you are given the assignment to discover how this policy can be carried out at minimum cost to the taxpayer. You would then look for the combination of resources — among all the possible combinations of teachers, specialist teachers, books, tapes, TV, and games — that is most efficient in teaching reading to particular types of children. It would not be an easy assignment if it were taken seriously.

Neither the businessman nor the school official has enough time to try out all possible combinations and to make an exhaustive comparison among them. What is needed is an efficient way to make decisions about efficient allocations of resources. And, just as in the case of the household that is trying to make decisions about what to consume, the economic logic comes to the rescue.

---

[3]If a corporation pursued a very aggressive antilabor policy and cut out all its institutional advertising and charitable contributions, it could probably increase its dividends in the current year, but it might thus impair its ability to earn profits in later years.

To consider again our businessman and his radios, it would be no great task for him to compute the extra, or marginal, output of radios for the last unit of each factor of production he might use. Let us call these values "marginal products." There will be a marginal product for each factor of production. For example, hiring one more foreman might raise the output by 200 radios a day. The trick is to allow only one factor to vary at a time and to consider the increment in output that is associated with a small change in the use of that factor. If the businessman can make this kind of computation for one factor, he can presumably do it for all the factors of production that he might employ. In addition, he should be able to estimate the cost (such as wage or salary, or depreciation and maintenance for machines) per day of each factor separately. When the ratios of marginal products to prices are equal, that is,

$$\frac{\text{MP of factor A}}{\text{Unit price of factor A}} = \frac{\text{MP of factor B}}{\text{Unit price of factor B}} = \cdots = \frac{\text{MP of factor N}}{\text{Unit price of factor N}}$$

then he will have achieved the most efficient allocation of resources.

To see why these ratios establish the most efficient combination of resources, imagine that the price per unit of each factor is $1. (This might be 1/40 of a machinist's daily wage, 1/200 of the daily cost of a lathe, and so on.) Now let us consider two factors only, labor and the machine, and let the marginal physical product of the last dollar spent on labor equal 9 radios, while the marginal physical product of the last dollar spent on the machine equals, say, 11 radios. Then

$$\frac{\text{MPP of labor}}{\text{Unit price of labor}} = \frac{9 \text{ radios}}{\$1} \neq \frac{11 \text{ radios}}{\$1} = \frac{\text{MPP of machines}}{\text{Unit price of machine}}$$

This is obviously not an ideal situation, because the firm could gain an increase in output of approximately 2 radios a day at zero money cost, or free, just by shifting a dollar's expenditure from labor to machines. By spending a dollar less on labor, the firm loses about 9 radios a day, but when it uses this dollar to increase its utilization of machines it increases its output by some 11 radios —a net gain of approximately 2. This process of shifting its resource allocation from labor to machines should continue until the marginal products per dollar are equal at, say, 10 radios per dollar of labor and 10 radios per dollar of machines. What applies to two factors also applies to many, so the overall efficient plan of production is the one in which all the ratios of marginal physical products to factor prices are equal. "Another way to say this is to say that the marginal contribution of a factor per dollar spent on it is the same for all factors of production."[4]

Now, how can we be sure that the marginal physical product will change so that when we use more or less of various factors we can indeed achieve a set of equal ratios. Here the economist relies on the *law of diminishing marginal productivity*, which corresponds to the law of diminishing marginal utility in the theory of household demand. The law of diminishing marginal productivity states that as we add more and more units of factor A while holding the use of all other factors (B, C, . . ., N) constant, we will receive ever smaller increments of product from the additional units of factor A. Suppose that on a large farm there are 10 tractors and 10 farmworkers, and that the number of farmworkers is increased to 11, then to 12, then to 13, and so on, but no adjustment is made in the number of acres in cultivation, number of tractors, and so on. Each successive worker added would reduce the average amount of land and machinery per employed person, and hence each successive worker would add something less to total output than the one hired just before him.

What applies to farms should apply to radio factories as well, so in our example above, the shift in resources from labor to machinery should, under the operation of the law of diminishing marginal productivity, raise the marginal product of labor from 9 radios toward 10 per dollar spent, and reduce the marginal product of machines from 11 toward 10 per dollar spent. Thus, as we move the allocation of resources in the "right direction" to achieve greater efficiency, the ratios of marginal products to price of factors draw closer together in value; hence the problem theoretically can be solved.

DEMAND SCHEDULES FOR FACTORS OF PRODUCTION

Let us look again at the set of ratios,

$$\frac{\text{MP of factor A}}{\text{Unit price of factor A}} = \frac{\text{MP of factor B}}{\text{Unit price of factor B}} = \cdots = \frac{\text{MP of factor N}}{\text{Unit price of factor N}}$$

and imagine that a manufacturer has succeeded in designing a plan of production so that all the ratios are equal. Suppose now that the price of factor A, expressed perhaps as an hourly wage rate, falls. What response would the manufacturer be expected to make? The ratio for factor A will now have a higher value than the other, because its denominator has been reduced. Clearly, the manufacturer should employ more of factor A, and as he does so

---

[4]Robert Dorfman, *The Price System* (Englewood Cliffs, N.J.: Prentice-Hall, 1964), p. 34.

the value of MP of factor A/unit price of factor A will gradually decline to its equilibrium position of equality with the ratios for the other factors. It will decline because the marginal product of factor A will decrease when more units of factor A are put in service. Just the opposite reaction would be appropriate if the price of factor A had gone up instead of down, that is, the manufacturer would reduce his employment of A. In reality it would often be true that the prices of several factors had changed at about the same time; hence the whole set of ratios would be in the process of adjustment. However, this analysis of factor A is sufficient to establish that the demand line for a factor of production slopes downward to the right, just as the household's demand line for goods and services does. As the price of a factor falls, employers will seek to make relatively greater use of it; as the price rises, employers will try to get along with less of it. This is a theoretical way of discussing actual events, because it is a matter of common observation that when a union has unusual success in bargaining for higher wages, the employer replaces the workers with machines. This has happened quite noticeably in coal mining.[5]

THE SUPPLY OF FACTORS OF PRODUCTION

Up to this point we have been mainly considering demand schedules, but now we must recognize that prices, including prices of factors of production (wages, salaries, fees, rent, interest on profits), are determined by conditions of supply as well as demand. Whatever the demand for some factor of production, the existence of bountiful quantities of it will probably dictate that the factor receive a rather low level of remuneration. Similarly, if a factor is in extremely limited supply, it may command a high price. Contrast the value of an acre of cutover timberland with an acre of business property in midtown Manhattan. Part of the difference in price is a result of the fact that old timberland exists in more plentiful supply than Manhattan real estate.

There are three broad classes of factors of production that the economist recognizes: labor, land, and capital (such as buildings and machinery). We shall concentrate on labor in discussing factor supply.

What is the nature of the general supply curve of labor? (Here labor is thought of as including all human services that are employed in the private

---

[5]The demand line for factors of production can shift upward or downward, just like the demand lines for consumers' goods. If an employer found that he could sell his product at a higher price now than he could last week, he might wish to raise the level of his productive activity. This means he would need to hire more factors of production and this in turn would represent an upward shift in the demand lines for those factors. How far would he expand his production, assuming he wants to make as much profit as possible? Up to the point where the additional (or marginal) cost of the last unit was just equal to the additional (or marginal) revenue that the last unit of product brought in. Stopping short of this point means less profit than he could have.

and public sectors of the economy.) To answer this question, we need to note how the quantity of human services employed might increase. There are three possibilities: (1) unemployed persons might find work; (2) persons not presently in the labor force (for example housewives, students, and retired people) might join it; and (3) persons in the labor force might be induced to work longer hours per week. The second and third sources of supply are normally the most significant in quantitative terms, and to draw additional persons into the labor force or to persuade people to work longer hours requires, generally speaking, a rise in the wages and salaries they can expect to receive. Accordingly, it is held that the general supply curve of labor slopes upward to the right.

Actually it is more interesting to think about the supply of particular kinds of labor: doctors as against teachers as against machinists, and so on. Fig. 1 shows two upward-sloping supply lines applying to Type A labor and Type B labor. The line is noticeably steeper for Type A than for Type B. Clearly this means that the supply of Type B labor is much more responsive to a change in wage or salary levels than Type A. For example, a given rise in wages, represented by the distance EF, leads to an increase in supply of Type B labor of distance RQ, which is considerably greater than the corresponding increase of Type A labor—MN. The economist describes the relation between factor price and factor supply by the concept of elasticity of supply:

$$\text{Elasticity of supply of labor} = \frac{\text{Percentage change in quantity of labor supplied}}{\text{Percentage change in wage (or salary) rates}}$$

Type A labor of Fig. 4 is characterized by relative inelasticity of supply, while Type B is relatively elastic.

FIG. 4
Two Labor Supply Schedules

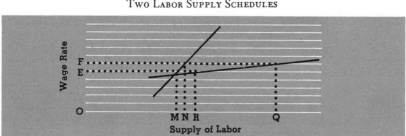

Supply of Labor

What conditions determine whether the supply of a particular type of labor will be relatively elastic or inelastic? Naturally enough, there are many conditions, but let us look at some of the major ones. (1) Some human skills, like the ability to sing opera, are rare. If there should be a rise in the demand for opera singers, one would not expect any great increase in their number— the number, that is, who could perform professionally in first-rate companies. So it is likely that the result of an increase in demand would be higher salaries for opera singers rather than a dramatic increase in the number of performers employed. (The higher salaries would serve to ration the limited number of top-grade performers among the richest and best-known opera companies.) Therefore natural scarcity of particular skills leads to inelastic supply. (2) Some occupations have higher entry standards than others. Contrast, for example, the standards of entry for practicing medicine and for teaching school. At the minimum, it takes about four more years of training, counting internship, to be a doctor than it does to be a teacher. On this count alone, short-run supply schedules for teachers would be expected to show greater elasticity than those of doctors. The economist would say that doctors and teachers are in "noncompeting labor groups," because no teacher can easily shift over and do the doctor's work.[6] (3) Certain occupations are basically either disagreeable or dangerous; others demand extreme patience, energy, or concentration. In these cases part of the wage or salary earned represents an "equalizing difference in pay"—an amount of extra money to offset the unattractiveness or the highly demanding nature of certain assignments.[7] Work in the "equalizing pay" category will generally be characterized by inelasticity of supply. Work that is pleasant and rather easy to do, but still of fairly high status, should on the contrary be characterized by elastic conditions of supply.

DEMAND AND SUPPLY DETERMINE PRICE

Fig. 5a includes a demand and a supply schedule on the same diagram. Let these represent demand and supply schedules for a factor of production, with the demand schedule being based on consideration of marginal productivity (discussed in the first part of this chapter) and the supply schedule

---

[6]On the other hand, it would not be appropriate to say that high school chemistry teachers and industrial chemists are in noncompeting groups.

[7]In England all primary and secondary teachers are paid under the same salary schedule (except those who work in London). It has been difficult to get sufficient numbers of teachers to go to the North of England, particularly to the old industrial and coal-mining areas. The English tackled the problem by placing quotas on the number of teachers each local authority could hire, thinking that if the favored authorities in the South were so limited, an extra number of teachers would more or less be forced to work in the North. An alternative approach would be to offer equalizing differences in pay to teachers who were willing to work in the difficult situations.

being related to the considerations we have mentioned in the preceding paragraphs. What will be the wage rate in this job market? The answer is given by the dollar amount represented by the distance QP_1, the distance QP_1 itself being determined by the intersection of the solid demand and supply lines. At any higher wage than QP_1, there will be more people offering themselves for work than employers would be willing to hire, and competition among the workers would force the wage rate down. At any lower wage, employers could not satisfy their desire to hire workers, and they would be led by competition to raise their wage offers. When the demand and supply schedules intersect, every employer who wishes to hire a worker at wage QP_1 can find a person to hire, and every worker who wishes to work at a wage of QP_1 can find a job. Thus there is no pressure to raise or lower the wage QP_1, once it is established, until there is a shift in either the demand or the supply schedule.

The dotted line on Fig. 5a represents an increase in demand. When such an increase occurs, the wage rate rises to QP_2 and the quantity of the given type of labor increases from PQ_1 to PQ_2. Fig. 5b portrays the same situation, except that the supply line of 5b is considerably more elastic than the one in 5a. The increase in demand now leads to a smaller rise in wages but a larger increase in employment. You might wish to experiment with demand and supply lines of varying degrees of elasticity, to see the effects of shifts in demand and supply lines under many conditions. You might also wish to consider the approximate shapes of demand and supply lines in the market for teachers' services and see how a shift in demand and supply would affect teachers' salaries and employment.

This method of determining price by noting the intersection of demand and supply schedules applies to markets for goods and services as well as to markets for factors of production. In Chapter 2 we discussed how demand schedules for goods and services can be derived. To construct supply schedules for goods, one starts with the supply schedules for factors of production and moves then to the determination of the most efficient combination of factors to produce specific goods, using marginal productivity analysis. It is assumed that supply schedules for goods slope upward to the right, because the schedules of supply for factors behave this way, and this means that cost of production will eventually go up as production expands. Market price is established at the point where demand and supply are equal.

In brief, consumer demand directs businessmen to produce those things that consumers most desire. Competition in product markets spurs businessmen to provide goods and services at low cost, that is, efficiently. Competition in factor markets assures that the incomes people receive are related to their (marginal) productivity. In its ideal workings, our decentralized economy performs in a manner both efficient and equitable.

FIG. 5 a

DETERMINATION OF WAGE RATE: LESS ELASTIC SUPPLY

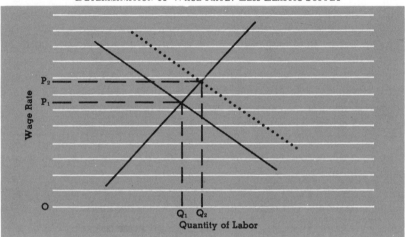

FIG. 5 b

DETERMINATION OF WAGE RATE: MORE ELASTIC SUPPLY

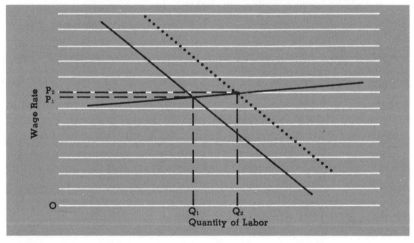

STABILITY IN SHARING THE NATIONAL PRODUCT

Before leaving the topic of returns to factors of production, let us note one rather unusual fact about the U.S. economy. Throughout the twentieth century the total share of the national product paid out in wages and salaries has consistently been three times as large as the share paid out to owners of property (profits, interest, and rent). Another way to state the relation is to say that a 1 percent increase in labor raises national output three times as much as a 1 percent increase in capital. Yet another way is to state that return to labor represents about three-quarters of the national product, and return to capital about one-quarter. And in spite of the tremendous changes that have occurred in our economy, this relation between labor and capital shares has held constant since the early 1900s.

The nature of the long-term changes in the supply of factors makes this constancy even more curious. Since the turn of the century "labor input" per capita, measured as man-hours worked, has held almost constant, but the amount of physical capital in use has increased at an annual rate of about 1.5 to 2.0 percent.[8] By the law of diminishing marginal productivity, it follows that the aggregate return to owners of property should have fallen, because capital has become relatively more plentiful and labor, correspondingly, has become relatively scarcer.

However, this comparison of the quantitative changes in the supply of capital and labor fails to take account of the possible improvements in quality. Business and government spend enormous sums on research and development ($100 billion during the decade 1953–63), and a substantial part of this expenditure has been for developing new and better types of capital equipment.[9] Expenditures on education can also be regarded as a means of improving the quality of labor. Indeed, it has been estimated that between 1910 and 1960, educational provision was responsible for a qualitative improvement equivalent to an increase in the quantity of labor of nearly 1 percent a year on the average.[10]

---

[8]The willingness of businessmen (and of those who provide investment funds to businessmen) to undertake projects to increase the supply of capital is influenced by many factors, including tax policy, the condition of international markets, changes in technology, and appraisal of the investment plans of their rivals. Choices between alternative investment projects are influenced by estimates of net return (revenues less costs attributable to a particular act of investment and the distribution of these returns over time.

[9]Indeed, it has now become the practice to speak of "generations" of capital equipment, with each successive generation distinguished from earlier ones by higher levels of performance capability. See Robert M. Solow, "Investment and Technical Progress." in Kenneth J. Arrow, Samuel Karlin, and Patrick Suppes, Mathematical Methods in the Social Sciences (Stanford, Calif.: Stanford Univ. Press, 1960), p. 91.

[10]Edward F. Denison, The Sources of Economic Growth in the United States and the Alternatives Before Us (New York: Committee for Economic Development, 1962). Also, a certain amount of education and training is provided in the work place. Just how much is not certain. Jacob Mincer ("On the Job Training: Costs, Returns, and Some Implications," Journal of Political Economy, October Supplement, 1962) suggests it may represent a value of $14 billion a year, but this figure includes informal as well as formal training, and it also includes the value of work experience in its broadest sense. On the other hand, the U.S. Department of Labor reports that only one manufacturing plant in five has a formal training program, and only about 1 percent of the manufacturing work force is enrolled in formal courses to learn specific skills.

Investigating changes in quality of factor inputs is a new interest of economists, and work has not gone far enough to indicate whether the supply of labor and the supply of capital have been increasing in step or not when qualitative change is taken into account. Therefore we do not know what these new findings will tell us about the constancy of factor shares. But this much is clear: the businessman is deadly serious about trying to improve the quality of those factor inputs that are under his control. One can suspect that industry has been far more successful than public services such as education in taking advantage of the opportunities that research offers for attaining a higher level of performance. The educational system distributes knowledge, but it has not yet done much to create new knowledge to serve its own needs, such as discovering the best techniques for teaching different children particular things at a given time. This kind of knowledge would allow a school district to make better choices in the allocation of its resources. It would know whether spending money to reduce class size in a particular grade would have greater effects on pupil achievement than spending the same money in raising teachers' salaries; it would know whether school breakfasts were more effective in reducing absenteeism than an improvement in the school playground would be. Often one is forced to make a choice between competing uses of money, and often the choice is made on the basis of nothing but sheer intuition.

Suggested Readings

BAUMOL, WILLIAM J. *Economic Theory and Operating Analysis.* Englewood Cliffs, N.J.: Prentice-Hall, 1961.

CAVES, RICHARD. *American Industry: Structure, Conduct, Performance.* Englewood Cliffs, N.J.: Prentice-Hall, 1964.

DORFMAN, ROBERT. *The Price System.* Englewood Cliffs, N.J.: Prentice-Hall, 1964.

DUNLOP, JOHN T. (ed.). *Automation and Technological Change.* Englewood Cliffs, N.J.: Prentice-Hall, 1962.

HENDERSON, JAMES M., and QUANDT, RICHARD E. *Microeconomic Theory: A Mathematical Approach.* New York: McGraw-Hill, 1958.

KENDRICK, J. W., and SATO, RYUSO. "Factor Prices, Productivity and Growth," *American Economic Review,* December 1963.

Chapter Four: THE ROLES OF GOVERNMENT

THE SCOPE OF PUBLIC ACTIVITIES

Between 1929 and 1962, expenditures at all levels of government in the United States rose by a factor of 16.5, from $10.2 billion to $168.5 billion. In 1929, public expenditures represented 9.8 percent of the gross national product, while by 1962 the share of government expenditures stood at 30.4 percent. The meaning of figures in the billions of dollars is rather vague for most of us, so it may be more descriptive to say that each man, woman, and child in the country now buys about $650 worth of public services each year and that a further $286 per person is redistributed among us in the form of veterans' benefits, social security payments, unemployment compensation, agricultural subsidies, interest on the public debt, and the like.

To understand why government has become so large, it is helpful to consider some of the bases for public expenditure.

1. *Collective Goods.* Let us think of national defense. This is a service provided by the central government. All citizens are defended from foreign

aggressors in more or less equal measure. If any individual should fail to pay his federal income tax, he would continue to receive the same measure of defense as other members of society, including those who managed to pay their taxes. The problem is that there is no way to exclude an individual from receiving defense services, once a defense establishment is created. If the responsibility of meeting the costs of defense were put on a voluntary basis, no individual (except on moral grounds, perhaps) would find it necessary to pay his share, because his share of total support would be so small that he would get about the same amount of protection whether he paid or not. A large defense program requires compulsory levies, otherwise known as taxes.

Another example of a collective good is a lighthouse. This aid to navigation casts its signals upon the water for all ships to use whether or not any individual shipowner makes a financial contribution toward its maintenance. National defense and lighthouses are rather pure examples of collective goods. Other services such as education often embody elements of both private and collective goods. For the individual, education offers such benefits as the opportunity to earn a higher salary and the opportunity to participate more fully in cultural activities. Theoretically, a person could be excluded from sharing in these advantages if he were unwilling to pay a fee for his schooling. For society as a whole, education offers certain social benefits. These are not related to the amount of fees — or taxes, for that matter — that an individual pays. In the United States, for example, he enjoys the benefits of living under a stable democratic government with a rising economic level; an educated populace is the basis for achieving this stability in government and these gains in productivity. No one can be excluded from the enjoyment of these social benefits.

2. *Zero Marginal Costs.* Some services have a marginal cost of operation (the cost per additional unit of service) of zero or almost zero. For example, the major maintenance costs for a bridge are generally unrelated to the amount of traffic it carries. Because no greater cost is incurred by allowing more motorists to use the bridge, there is no point in discouraging its use by charging a toll. In fact, only by making the bridge toll-free can the ratio of benefits to costs be maximized, because the total benefit to the community would be increased every time the bridge was used. To maximize benefits, one must maximize use.

If a private company were financing the bridge, obviously it would have to charge a toll to recover its original investment and make a profit. On the other hand, if a government were financing the bridge, it could sell bonds to obtain the funds and then pay off the debt by levying taxes on all the people in the area, or perhaps just on those who owned cars or trucks. In this way a government could avoid charging tolls and it could maximize the use of the bridge. The case of zero marginal costs is another basis for government intervention in the economy.

3. *Natural Monopolies.* The production of some goods and services is less expensive if all the work is done by one company than if there are several companies competing for the consumers' attention. If several companies tried to produce and distribute electric power in the same part of a city, each would need to invest in light poles, wiring, transformers, and other equipment, and the result would be wasteful duplication. In cases of natural monopoly like this, the government may choose to leave the business in the hands of a single private company, but it would probably exercise some control over the prices that the company charges its consumers, as it does over rates for telephone service. In other instances the government may choose to provide the service itself, as in the case of our mail service.

4. *High-Risk Ventures.* The expenditure of large sums of money and the acceptance of considerable financial risk are necessary for certain programs such as the development of a supersonic airliner or a process for desalinating water, or the search for improved pedagogy through educational research. These kinds of research call for the exploration of many possibilities that will ultimately turn out to be dead ends. It may be appropriate for the government to meet at least part of the cost of these high-risk ventures.

5. *Redistribution of Income.* Advanced societies are concerned about reducing poverty. Government in these societies provides various kinds of welfare payments, finances public housing projects, and offers public health services.

6. *Stabilization of the Economy.* Ever since the 1930s the federal government has assumed the responsibility for minimizing violent swings of the economy from deep depression to runaway inflation. This responsibility was formally recognized in the Employment Act of 1946. In the next chapter we will consider some of the means that the government uses to promote stability.

The list of bases for public activity could of course be extended. However, enough has been said to enable you to make your own analysis of why government expenditures have increased so greatly, taking into account such exogenous factors as the cold war, population expansion, and the technological revolution.[1]

GOVERNMENT FINANCING VS. GOVERNMENT OPERATION

In general, the bases for government intervention establish a stronger case for public financing of activities than for public operation of them. Actually, many things that are paid for by taxation, such as highways, dams, and schoolhouses, are produced by private firms. The equipment used for fire and

---

[1]For a more complete statement, see John F. Due, *Government Finance* (Homewood, Ill.: Richard D. Irwin, 1954), Chap. 1.

police protection is produced privately, and research in many fields is conducted by both state and private universities under government contract.

It is interesting to note that an economist at the University of Chicago, Professor Milton Friedman, has suggested that the financing of schools should remain largely public, but that the near monopoly of state and local governments in the administration of elementary and secondary schools should be reduced.[2] Specifically, he has proposed that each household be eligible to receive a voucher equal in value to the per-pupil cost of education in the local district, which could be applied toward tuition fees in any school approved by the state authorities. The expansion of private education, it is claimed, would have certain economic benefits: households could choose the amount of educational services they consume (above a minimum set by the state), and the private institutions would attain a higher level of efficiency because they would be subject to the pressure of competition. You might wish to evaluate the case for such a shift toward private administration of the educational services.[3]

SOURCES OF PUBLIC REVENUE

Governments obtain revenue in an enormous variety of ways: from fees for court, postal, water, light, and transit services; from royalties for the lease of mineral rights on public lands; from short- and long-term loans; and from a variety of taxes. In the past more than now, governments have even obtained revenue by simply ordering a new batch of paper money printed. However, the one dominant general source of funds is taxation; even when governments borrow money, they create the necessity for higher taxes in the future to meet the interest payments on the debt.

There are three main bases for taxation. One is income; taxes are levied both on personal (or household) income and on the income of corporations. The second is the amount of money a person spends on ordinary goods and services; levies on spending are collected through sales and excise taxes. The third basis is the amount of wealth a person owns; collections are made through property, gift, and estate taxes. The federal government relies most heavily on personal income and corporation income taxes. The predominant source of revenue for the state is the general sales tax, but states use a wide variety of levies, including various kinds of income taxes. Indeed, some states forgo the use of the general sales tax and rely upon income taxes as much as the federal

---

[2]Milton Friedman, "The Role of Government in Education," in *Economics and the Public Interest*, ed. Robert A. Solo (New Brunswick, N.J.: Rutgers Univ. Press, 1955), pp. 123–42.

[3]For arguments against Professor Friedman's position, see John Vaizey, *The Economics of Education* (London: Faber & Faber, 1962), pp. 28–36.

government does. At the local level, things are really very simple (except in the large cities, which are authorized to use an assortment of taxes); localities are generally restricted to a tax on private property.

Economists have tried to establish criteria for judging whether particular taxes are good or bad. One of these criteria is equity. To be equitable, the tax must treat equally persons who are equal in relevant aspects. Two men who have the same amount of income and the same number of dependents should be required to pay income tax in approximately equal amounts. If you and your friend walk into a store and buy the same article, you should not be allowed to pay only half the amount of sales tax that was collected from your friend.

In our modern complex economy, even such a simple rule as "equal treatment of equals" is not always easy to apply, but things get much worse when we raise the question of how "unequals" should be treated. If one man has twice the income of another, how much more tax should be levied on the richer man than on the poorer? If each pays the same percentage of his income in tax, we have a case of *proportional* taxation. If the rich man pays a larger percentage of income in tax than the poorer one, this is described as *progressive* taxation, because the rate of tax progresses upward as the income to be taxed goes up. Some taxes, like the property tax, are somewhat *regressive*. That is, the poorer households pay a higher percentage of tax than the rich.[4] For the most part, economists prefer that taxes be progressive, because they feel it is fairer. But there is no real scientific basis for establishing exactly how much more rich families should pay. Accordingly, the rising schedule of federal income tax rates is determined by political compromise, not on the basis of how the utility schedules of different households are affected by particular rate structures.[5]

Tax instruments can also be judged on their "economic neutrality." A tax should not have an unintended effect on the choices that people make. For example, if the rate structure of a progressive income tax discouraged people from working hard, it would not be economically neutral.[6] In addition,

---

[4]The primary reason the property tax is somewhat regressive is that over half of the revenue is drawn from the levy on residential property. In some local governments, including school districts, the amount derived from this levy may even exceed 80 percent. Because rich families spend a somewhat smaller proportion of their income on housing than poor ones, the property tax will naturally tend to be regressive.

[5]When the levies of all levels of government in the United States are considered as a whole, the taxation appears to be slightly progressive. This is mainly because the progressive federal income taxes outweigh the slightly regressive state and local taxes. See R. A. Musgrave, "The Incidence of the Tax Structure and Its Effects on Consumption," in *Federal Tax Policy for Economic Growth and Stability*, Joint Economic Committee (Washington: Government Printing Office, 1955), p. 98.

[6]For a study of this problem, see George F. Break, "Income Taxes and Incentive to Work: An Empirical Study," *American Economic Review*, September 1957.

a tax on any commodity or service will ordinarily reduce its consumption. When an excise is placed on cigarettes or liquor, the curtailment of consumption that results may be regarded as socially desirable. But when a property tax, which is actually a rather substantial excise, is placed on housing, any reduction in consumption could hardly be considered socially desirable. Therefore the property tax is also a departure from economic neutrality.

The other criteria for judging taxation can be stated more briefly. The tax should be definite and predictable in amount. It should be easily enforceable and acceptable to the public. Collection of the tax should not involve excessive expense. It should not place an onerous burden of special legal and accounting costs on the taxpayer. Lastly, the tax should produce revenue for the government that levied it.

The progressive federal income taxes are highly responsive to changes in income. For example, a 1 percent increase in national income leads to a revenue increase of approximately 1.5 percent. Thus, in good times the federal government finds its revenue expanding automatically. The property tax—the mainstay of public school finance—is not automatically responsive in the same degree, and the rates have to be raised periodically to raise the needed revenue.[7] If you have concluded that there is no ideal tax, you are right! This is one reason the United States employs such a variety of tax instruments; extreme reliance on any single one could have harmful economic consequences.

EXPENDITURES AND REVENUES

The federal government carries the major responsibilities for defense, agricultural support, development of national resources, space research, and international affairs, including foreign aid. The biggest block of expenditure at the state level is for highways, but states also have important responsibilities for hospitals, community redevelopment, higher education, and a variety of welfare programs. Local governments are responsible for administering elementary and secondary schools (their biggest job), providing police and fire protection, maintaining the streets, and supervising local welfare programs. These are some major types of expenditures administered at every level of government.

Potentially, the federal government can raise more revenue than the state and local governments, because it has more effective tax instruments. Similarly,

---

[7]However, the record of the property tax in producing revenue in the postwar period is quite remarkable, because so far people have been willing to accept substantial rate increases. A recent study in New York State shows that property tax collection, on the average, increased 1.6 percent for each 1 percent rise in county income. See Jesse Burkhead, *Public School Finance* (Syracuse, N. Y.: Syracuse Univ. Press, 1964), p. 188.

state governments can often raise money more easily than local ones. Consequently there is a lack of correlation between the revenue requirements of a government and its ability to raise funds from its own tax sources. For this reason, the federal government distributes about $8 billion a year to state and local governments, especially for highways and welfare payments, and the state governments distribute an additional $11 billion a year from their tax revenues to the local governments, mainly for education. The states provide about 40 percent of the elementary and secondary school revenues, and the federal share is rapidly rising toward 10 percent. Only about half of school revenues are raised from local tax sources.

Grant-in-aid formulas are ordinarily used to compute the revenue required by a government for a specific expenditure. For example, the educational expenditures of a local school district are commonly computed by multiplying the number of children in attendance in public school by the average per-pupil cost in the state. Many formulas also take into account the fiscal ability of the receiving government to meet its needs from its own tax resources. A poor district (or state) will receive a larger share of its funds from the higher government than will a rich one. In 1962 the relatively rich state of Connecticut received only 10.7 percent of its state and local expenditures from the federal government, while Alabama got 24.1 percent. In your state you can probably find school districts that receive 75 percent or more of their revenue from state and federal grants, while richer districts may be getting only about 15 percent. But in spite of these adjustments, many of the poorer state and local governments have to tax themselves heavily to provide programs that are still far below the standards set in rich communities. Later on we shall consider whether the administration of school services should be moved closer to the sources of local revenue or centralized at the state or federal level.

DISTRIBUTION OF PUBLIC BENEFITS

To achieve the proper distribution of public services is an even thornier problem than to achieve a proper distribution of the tax burden. The same rule about equal treatment of equals should apply: all people of similar need should have the same opportunity to use public services. This does not always happen. There is some evidence, for example, that the Agricultural Extension Service formerly gave special attention to farmers who were "already favored in education, intelligence, and perhaps, good fortune."[8] In your state you can probably find school districts of extremely limited taxable resources that offer meager programs while taxing their citizens at high rates, as well as rich

---

[8]Grant McConnell, The Decline of Agrarian Democracy (Berkeley: Univ. of California Press, 1953), p. 163.

districts that finance lavish programs at relatively low tax rates. Since the tax rate is a kind of price for educational services, citizens of the poorer districts are paying a discriminatorily high price for educational services.

An even more difficult problem to resolve is how to treat unequals. Educational resources are not unlimited, and they should be allocated according to the ability and aptitude of the pupils. Should bright children be favored at the expense of the less bright? In the post-Sputnik years some states have apparently answered affirmatively. But now we recognize that measured ability may deceive, that children may only appear to be "less bright"—perhaps because their homes were inimical to intellectual development. So now, at least, some special attention is being given to children from "culturally deprived" homes. We are still not seriously trying to foster the abilities of the slow learner (as distinct from the mentally retarded), but conceivably this should become an important social objective.

EFFICIENCY IN THE PUBLIC SECTOR

Theoretically, the economic logic should apply as well to public activities as it does to private. That is, the last dollar spent on each different type of public service should yield equal satisfaction to the consumer. The marginal expenditure on education, for example, should offer returns equal to the marginal expenditure on highways. Likewise, the last dollar spent in the public sector should return the same volume of satisfaction as the last dollar spent in the private sector, which means that the marginal expenditure on schools should be equated with the marginal expenditure on movies, smoked salmon, and all the rest. Finally, each public activity should function at maximum efficiency—the output should be produced at least cost.

There are reasons to doubt that these optimum conditions prevail. In the first place, in order for a service to be offered, (a) it must have the support of a fairly large group and (b) it must not be vetoed by any group. The desires of isolated individuals or controversial groups are likely to be shunted aside. Second, the quantity of public services is often decided in legislatures through political compromise, which is not wholly satisfactory in making fine marginal decisions. At other times decisions are made by a vote, such as a school tax referendum. Once the voters decide on a level of expenditure, all the citizens in the district receive the same amount of services (or have it offered to them whether they choose to participate or not). Some citizens—parents, perhaps— might prefer a higher expenditure, while others, such as retired people, might want less. It is possible that no one will be really satisfied with the outcome. In contrast, when one enters a private market, he may satisfy himself by buying just the amount of each commodity that pleases him.

The efficiency of government services is difficult to measure in quantitative terms. It is not easy to tell how much education has been produced in a given year in a school district, for example. This makes it difficult to evaluate the significance of changes in the volume of inputs. If teachers receive a raise in pay, was there an improvement in educational services, or could the district have obtained an even greater improvement by using the money to hire additional teachers and reduce class size? These questions are hard to answer when the product cannot be measured exactly.

But many private companies that supply services have similar difficulties in measuring their output. However, private companies may be guided by their profits. If a change in the pattern of inputs results in higher profits, it is assumed that the new pattern is more efficient. Governments lack this final, conclusive measurement of economic effectiveness to help them make their production decisions.

But one should not be pessimistic. A great deal can be accomplished in government by making precise delegations of authority, by defining objectives closely, by exploring alternative means for accomplishing objectives, and by making choices between different means on the basis of relative cost. In education, it is likely that the potential of productivity has only begun to be explored. As research in education expands, we may make advances similar to those scored in medicine, agriculture, and the physical sciences.

Suggested Readings

BENSON, CHARLES S. *The Economics of Public Education.* Boston: Houghton Mifflin, 1961.

BURKHEAD, JESSE. *Public School Finance: Economics and Politics.* Syracuse, N.Y.: Syracuse Univ. Press, 1964.

DUE, JOHN F. *Government Finance: An Economic Analysis.* 3d ed. Homewood, Ill.: Richard D. Irwin, 1963.

ECKSTEIN, OTTO. *Public Finance.* Englewood Cliffs, N.J.: Prentice-Hall, 1964.

JOHNS, ROE L., and MORPHET, EDGAR L. *Financing the Public Schools.* Englewood Cliffs, N.J.: Prentice-Hall, 1960.

MUSGRAVE, RICHARD. *The Theory of Public Finance.* New York: McGraw-Hill, 1959.

Chapter Five: FEDERAL POLICIES FOR ECONOMIC STABILIZATION AND GROWTH

From the end of World War II until the early months of the Johnson administration, the government's activities in the economy could be compared to those of a suburban fire company going into action only when someone reports a fire or a broken water main. In this period (1945–64) the government limited itself largely to offsetting recessions or price inflation. We shall discuss some of the techniques that were used.

In the first year of the Johnson administration a new and more pervasive policy was accepted; the government was to urge the economy toward its potential level of output. Waste in unemployed manpower and underemployed capital equipment was to be exorcised. Then the federal government began to explore the next major policy adventure—raising the potential output itself by taking measures to increase the share of resources devoted to investment and research, by seeking in bold new ways to strengthen the schools, and by spreading knowledge about the best technologies in civilian production. Through these measures the central authority hoped to promote a rise in productivity (or output per man-hour).

FISCAL POLICY AND NATIONAL INCOME DETERMINATION

To help us understand the old and the new in economic policy, we need to consider the main outlines of the theory of "national income determination," which is the explanation of the forces that set the level of economic activity in a country. The theory was developed chiefly by one man, the late J. M. Keynes, an English economist.

Let us start by thinking of an economy in which all production and consumption are in private hands—an economy in which there is no government activity. Suppose the business firms produce goods equal in value to $450 billion (at current prices). How do they know that purchasers will buy just that amount of goods?[1] The answer is that they don't. If the households of the land feel an urge to increase the volume of their savings, there will be a shortfall in demand and unwanted goods will pile up on retailers' shelves, in warehouses, and in the shipping rooms of factories. The natural response of businessmen will be to reduce their level of output in order to halt the pileup of unsold goods. Essentially, they will attempt to stop their losses. This means that workers will be laid off and, correspondingly, that the level of national income will fall.

On the other hand, suppose that households are feeling quite expansive during a particular year. They spend their current income and also buy many goods on credit (installment plans, bank loans, "go-now-pay-later" schemes, etc.). The business firms cannot immediately supply the extra goods that consumers want, and after warehouse stocks are reduced to minimum levels, prices rise. Consumers spend their earned and borrowed money, but they of course cannot have more goods than are available to buy. The gap between the volume of spending and the supply of things to purchase results in an inflationary rise in the price level; consumers are charged more for the available supply.

Even from these introductory remarks you can probably see that the level of national income is somewhat unstable. It moves around a bit from time to time, and the exact level at which we would achieve the combination of full employment and price stability is only one point on a recession-inflation spectrum. Actually, the theory of income determination goes on to state that there is no natural force in the private economy to bring the economic system to that ideal point and hold it there.

For expository purposes, we have so far been talking as if the only people who buy goods are members of households. This, of course, is not so. Business firms represent a major market for the output of this economy, and when they

---

[1]The money, of course, is available to buy the $450 billion worth of goods, because when goods are produced an equivalent amount of factor income (wages, salaries, interest, rent, dividends) is distributed, as we noted in the last part of Chapter 1.

purchase new machines and build new factories, their purchases are called investments. Similarly, when business firms increase the size of their inventories, this also is described as investment. (We know, of course, that government spending bulks large in our economy. Government purchases of goods and services are as important in national income determination as business investment is; we shall consider this complexity shortly.) Household consumption purchases ordinarily bear a stable relation to household income. Taking all households together, we find that they spend approximately 90 percent of their current income year in and year out. But investment expenditures by business firms are quite volatile, and it is the changes in the volume of investment that are most likely to move the economy from recession to boom and back again.

At any time the economy can be said to be searching for an equilibrium position, a position in which the volume of national output (or its equivalent, income) is just equal to aggregate demand. In a way this search for an equilibrium position is similar to the determination of wages or other kinds of prices in the various markets that make up our total economy, as discussed on pages 29-35. The equilibrium position of national income represents an intersection of a schedule of supply (aggregate output) and demand (aggregate expenditure). The point of intersection is reached when the volume of business and personal savings is just matched by the volume of investment that is made by business firms and long-term household investment, such as residential construction. The following arithmetical example is helpful in understanding the equilibrium level of income.

If business firms had planned on an output of $400 billion, given the relationships in Table I, they would have found that they had undershot the mark. The total of consumption demand and investment demand would have been $20 billion greater than their planned output. Inventories would fall and prices would probably rise, at least to some extent. To restore the proper level of inventories and to take advantage of the chance to make a profit in a rising market, the firms would expand their operations (hire more workers, etc.) and gross national product would rise. At the level of $450 GNP, there is an equality of planned output and total purchases. Note that this is the output at which total savings ($60 billion) is just equal to investment, so the gap in spending created by the households' determination to save part of their income is exactly filled by the spending on machines, factories, and the like. At this point there is no pressure on the business firms to either expand or contract their level of operations, and we have arrived at the equilibrium level of income.

As a further exercise, you may want to start with a planned output level of $600 billion and consider how the excess of savings over investment leads to a decline in GNP, down to the equilibrium level of $450 billion.

TABLE I[2]

EQUILIBRIUM LEVEL OF GROSS NATIONAL PRODUCT: FIRST CASE

1	2	3	4	5
GNP (Output) = GNI (Income)	Consumption Demand	Investment Demand	Total Purchases (Aggregate Demand, Col. 2 + Col. 3)	Total Savings (Col. 1 — Col. 2)
300	300	60	360	0
350	330	60	390	20
400	360	60	420	40
*450	390	60	450	60
500	420	60	480	80
550	450	60	510	100
600	480	60	540	120

*Equilibrium

Businessmen do not have perfect foresight, however, and hence one cannot expect the planned level of production always to coincide with the equilibrium of GNP. Moreover, the economy receives shocks from the outside, such as large-scale strikes and rumors of war, that may move the economy off its established equilibrium. Even the existence of a theoretical equilibrium position for an economy does not in itself guarantee that economic stability will be achieved. Referring to Table I again, suppose that at the existing levels of resources and technology, the maximum output of the economy at current prices were $400 billion. The equilibrium position of $450 would represent a condition of persistent inflation. In addition, if full employment of the labor force would occur only when an output level of $600 had been reached, the equilibrium level of $450 GNP would represent a persistent state of unemployment, somewhat like the one that has existed in the United States since 1958. Therefore the equilibrium level of output does not necessarily coincide with the attainment of the potential output of the economy and with price stability.

You will note in Table I that the volume of consumption moves upward in a regular fashion as GNP increases. It is a fundamental assumption in economics that total consumption is determined rather precisely by the magnitude of national product; this assumption is supported by considerable empirical evidence. It follows that the volume of savings is also determined by the size of GNP, since savings are defined as the difference between GNP and

---

[2]This table is similar to the one presented in Charles L. Schultze, *National Income Analysis* (Englewood Cliffs, N.J.: Prentice-Hall, 1964), p. 52. In this table and the three that follow, the figures are chosen for expository purposes; they do not represent accurately the actual magnitude of consumption, investment, and other factors relative to gross national product.

consumption. (At low levels of national income, such as the $300 billion level in Table I, savings can disappear, because people must use all their income to sustain life.) Investment, on the other hand, shows no close relation to changes in GNP *in the short run.* Table I indicates how the equilibrium level of income is reached when the volume of investment happens to be $60 billion a year.

Investment spending is a dynamic element in our economy, however, and the volume of investment can and does change quite sharply. Table II shows what happens to our hypothetical economy when the volume of investment rises to $80 billion.

TABLE II

EQUILIBRIUM LEVEL OF GROSS NATIONAL PRODUCT: SECOND CASE

1	2	3	4	5
GNP (Output) = GNI (Income)	Consumption Demand	Investment Demand	Total Purchases (Aggregate Demand, Col. 2 + Col. 3)	Total Savings (Col. 1 — Col. 2)
300	300	80	380	0
350	330	80	410	20
400	360	80	440	40
450	390	80	470	60
*500	420	80	500	80
550	450	80	530	100
600	480	80	560	120

*Equilibrium

The equilibrium level of income goes up to $500 billion. At this point total output equals total purchases, and the sum of dollars spent in investment is equal to the sum of dollars saved. But note that GNP increased by $50 billion while investment rose by only $20 billion! Each dollar of investment spending, in other words, led to a gain in GNP of $2.50. This relation between a change in investment and the expansion or contraction of GNP is called the "multiplier." The operation of the multiplier is illustrated in the following example.

If businessmen increase their expenditures on plant and equipment by $20 billion, the bulk of the money may be paid in wages and salaries to people who work in machine tool plants or in construction firms. They will probably spend the major portion of their incomes to buy groceries, clothing, TV sets, and so on. But the chain of spending does not stop with this first round. The retailers who serve them will also enjoy a rise in income and they also will spend most of their extra earnings on consumer goods. Indeed, the initial increase in investment sets off an infinite series of increments in consumption spending, although the increments become progressively smaller with each round. For example, if people spend an average of 60 percent of the increase in income they receive, the series of increments of a $20 billion increase in investment is as follows:

Operation of Multiplier: Increase in Consumption Spending

Initial investment	$20.0 billion
First round of respending	12.0
Second round of respending	7.2
Third round of respending	4.3
. . .	. . .
Tenth round of respending	0.1
Eleventh round of respending	0.06

In each instance the figures for respending were obtained by applying the ratio of 6/10 to the change in consumption spending in the preceding round. The sum of these increments will approach a limit of $50 billion. A permanent rise in investment of $20 billion would increase the level of GNP by $50 billion. The gain in GNP is 2½ times the increase in investment; therefore the multiplier has a value of 2½.[3]

We are now ready to drop our convenient assumption that the economy consists only of private activities. The role of government in national income determination can be illustrated by the familiar type of table. Table III indicates that the government has annual expenditures of $40 billion at all levels when GNP is $300 (column 4). Government expenditures represent a form of purchase similar to private investment demand; therefore total purchases (column 5) are the sum of consumption, private investment, and government expenditures. We have assumed in this example that private investment was maintained at the level of the example in Table II.

Ordinarily, of course, governments levy taxes as well as make expenditures. In their effect on national income, taxes correspond to savings; they offset spending. They also depress the level of national income. Column 7 shows the amount of taxes that might be levied by a government. Note that the taxes increase as GNP increases, in both absolute and relative terms; this would be the expected result under a progressive system of taxation.

As an example, let us make two assumptions: (1) that taxes are levied only on households, and (2) that the households maintain their previous levels of

---

[3]Basically, the magnitude of the multiplier depends on how households allocate income between consumption and savings. If they are inclined to save only a small proportion of any extra income they receive, the value of the multiplier could be quite high, even as high as 8 or 9. Much effort is devoted to empirical studies that will estimate the values of multipliers; the values used by government economists range from 2½ to 4.

TABLE III

Equilibrium Level of Gross National Product: Third Case

1	2	3	4	5	6	7
GNP (Output) = GNI (Income)	Consumption Demand	Investment Demand	Government Expenditures	Total Purchases (Aggregate Demand, Col. 2 + Col. 3 + Col. 4)	Total Savings [Col. 1 — (Col. 2 + Col. 7)]	Taxes
300	300	80	0	380	0	0
350	320	80	40	440	20	10
400	340	80	40	460	40	20
450	360	80	40	480	60	30
*500	380	80	40	500	80	40
550	400	80	40	520	100	50
600	420	80	40	540	120	60

*Equilibrium

savings. The second assumption means that people find the money to pay their taxes by forgoing purchases rather than by reducing savings. You can see how this affects the volume of consumption by comparing column 2 of Table III with column 2 of Table II.

What is the equilibrium level in Table III? It is $500 billion, the level of income at which GNP is equal to aggregate demand. At this level of GNP the sum of private investment and government expenditures, $120 billion, is just equal to the sum of savings and taxes. Private investment and government expenditures exert an upward pressure on GNP, but at the $500 billion mark their upward force is exactly offset by savings and taxes.[4]

Just as a shift in the volume of private investment leads to a change in the equilibrium level of GNP, so also does a shift in the volume of government spending. Suppose the government, leaving taxes unchanged, increased its spending by $20 billion. If the multiplier is 2½, GNP would rise by $50 billion.

A somewhat more interesting example, a tax cut, is shown in Table IV. Comparing column 7 of Table IV with the same column in Table II, you can see that the government has adopted a new, lower schedule of taxes. The money not taken in taxes can be used for consumption spending. Therefore the tax cut should lead to a higher level of GNP. The equilibrium level in Table IV is $550, $50 higher than the equilibrium level in Table III. After the tax cut, households are paying $20 billion less in taxes, raising the GNP by $20 billion as the expansion in private investment did in our earlier examples.

[4]Governments, especially the federal government, have the power to make decisions on expenditures and taxation somewhat independently of each other. If the federal government decides to increase its expenditures, it does not have to raise taxes at the same time. Instead it can borrow from banks to obtain any cash it requires, and it has one major lender of last resort, the Federal Reserve banking system.

TABLE IV

EQUILIBRIUM LEVEL OF GROSS NATIONAL PRODUCT: FOURTH CASE

GNP (Output) = GNI (Income)	Consumption Demand	Investment Demand	Government Expenditure	Total Purchases (Aggregate Demand, Col. 2 + Col. 3 + Col. 4)	Total Savings [Col. 1 — (Col. 2 + Col. 7)]	Taxes
300	300	80	0	380	0	0
350	330	80	40	450	20	0
400	355	80	40	475	40	5
450	380	80	40	500	60	10
500	405	80	40	525	80	15
*550	430	80	40	550	100	20
600	455	80	40	575	120	25

*Equilibrium

POTENTIAL OUTPUT AND TAX CUTS

In the economic annals of the United States, 1964 will be known as the year of the tax cut. Early in that year personal income tax liabilities were reduced by $6.7 billion, and corporate profits tax liabilities by $1.7 billion. Further reductions made effective in 1965 raised these reductions to $11 billion and $3 billion. In March 1964 withholding rates on wages and salaries were reduced from 18 to 14 percent, which actually was the reduction called for under the 1964 and 1965 tax cuts combined. The tax cut added $7.7 billion directly to disposable income in 1964 and, taking into account the multiplier (estimated by the Council of Economic Advisers to have a value of approximately 2), it caused a rise in consumer spending of $13 billion by the end of the year. In 1965 the continuing operation of the multiplier was expected to raise consumer spending about $18 billion above what it would have been without the tax cut. Between 1963 and 1964 the growth rate in GNP was 4.5, with the actual GNP rising to $622 billion in 1964.

These figures refer to only one period in our economic history, and they are therefore relatively unimportant. What is important is that the federal government has accepted the responsibility for pursuing a vigorous fiscal policy in a time of general prosperity and price stability.[5] There was no economic emergency in sight when the tax cut was passed; indeed, it was

[5]English and European economists have complained in recent years that the United States has lagged in adopting policies to promote the full utilization of its resources. For example, Angus Maddison, an economist long associated with the Organization for Economic Cooperation and Development in Paris, wrote in 1964: "The United States has . . . a good deal to learn from Europe in the art of economic management. It particularly needs to develop an active fiscal policy." Economic Growth in the West (New York: Twentieth Century Fund, 1964), p. 19. It is doubtful that such a criticism could be made today.

passed with the objective, not of forestalling disaster, but of urging the economy upward to its potential level of output.

As we have just seen, the federal government can stimulate economic activity by raising its expenditures or by reducing taxes. Tax cuts have special appeal. They can be quickly applied. They are flexible because they can be applied even when there is no urgent need for raising the level of federal expenditures. They are acceptable to people who fear the steady encroachment of federal programs on the private domestic economy. In the future, nonetheless, we shall surely see some increase in federal expenditures. After all, at high levels of economic activity, the federal tax system produces an extra $6 to $7 billion in revenue each year. Part of this extra money will doubtless be used to expand federal programs in education, research, the development of natural resources, and the improvement of urban life. Part of it will be returned to the consumer in tax cuts. Another part will be available, if desired, for distribution to state governments as block grants to strengthen our federal system of government.

We have passed into a time of buoyant expectations about the role of economics in maintaining prosperity and in promoting the balanced growth of our system of production. Part of the credit for this buoyancy rightly belongs to the economic advisers of the government who by skillful judgment and analysis were able to make extremely close predictions about the effects of a prosperity tax cut. Part of the credit, on the other hand, belongs to the businessmen and labor leaders who have exercised restraint in price and wage increases. Without such restraint, the tax cut could have been dissipated in inflation.

THE COMPLEXITY OF ECONOMIC GROWTH

Keeping actual output up to potential is the aim of the federal government's fiscal policy. Expanding the frontier of potential output is a larger and more complex task. It is one which involves all levels of government and many private firms and agencies. In a sense we have always been concerned with economic growth, but the intensive pursuit of productivity-increasing policies by the federal government is something new on the scene.

Before we consider some specific directions of policy, we should pause to note the large number of variables that affect potential output. These range from the health and morale of the working population to the rewards offered to businessmen for their risks, and from the effectiveness of antitrust legislation and patent policy to the prestige accorded scientists for discovery of new techniques of production. The variables also include such factors as the size of markets, the geographic mobility of labor, and the willingness of workers to accept technological change. In addition, the methods used to develop the skills of the work force are especially important. Enough has been said about the variables that affect productivity so that you can draw up your own list. Yours should be as good as or better than any economist's, because the economist tends to restrict himself to variables that can be cast in quantitative form.

POLICIES TO RAISE THE OUTPUT POTENTIAL

The federal government is following a multifaceted approach to the problem of raising the output potential. It is seeking better economic criteria for the interpretation of antitrust legislation; it is endeavoring to strengthen competition in the transportation industry; it is attempting to obtain coordination in the generation and distribution of electric power. There are, however, three major activities in the government's program for economic advancement: (1) The government offers tax inducements (in particular, credits under the corporate income tax laws) to industry for expanding the volume of its investments in physical capital, on the assumption that the new vintages of capital will be more productive than the old. (2) The government promotes research and innovation. It conducts its own research to assist civilian technology in the fields of water desalination, supersonic air transportation, and urban mass transportation. It also finances basic research, much of which has civilian as well as military applications, in the universities. In addition, by providing grants for the construction of university facilities and for scholarships and fellowships, it is attempting to increase the future supply of scientists and research workers. (3) To help future members of the labor force acquire the skills they will need in a technological age, the government is assuming a larger role in supporting elementary and secondary schools. This policy is implemented through the National Defense Education Act, the Vocational Education Act of 1963, and the Elementary and Secondary School Education Act of 1965.

POLICIES TO WIDEN THE CIRCLE OF AFFLUENCE

The government is pursuing policies to raise the level of national income through its programs for depressed areas such as Appalachia and through the upgrading of public services in poor neighborhoods (Economic Opportunity Act of 1964). But these policies have the more specific aim of enabling people to rise out of poverty. The need for special programs was well stated by Professor Walter Heller, formerly chairman of the Council of Economic Advisers:

> "The new tax cut will sharply step up our rate of economic growth. By creating 2 to 3 million new jobs, it will open exits from poverty at a faster pace. But open exits mean little to those who cannot move — to the millions who are caught in the web of poverty through illiteracy, lack of skills, racial discrimination, broken homes, and ill health — conditions which are hardly touched by prosperity and growth.

"A surprisingly large percentage of poor persons already have some kind of job. . . . The cause of poverty here is not lack of jobs but lack of higher skills and productivity needed to yield a decent income. As the demand for labor rises, many part-time or laid-off earners will receive higher wages. But most of the poor earners already have full-time employment, and added jobs will not help. They must be equipped with the knowledge, skills, and health to find and hold better jobs."[5]

Clearly, education is a key instrument in widening the circle of affluence, just as it is in raising the potential level of output of our economy. In Chapter 6 we turn to a detailed consideration of the role of education in our productive system.

Suggested Readings

ACKLEY, GARDNER. Macroeconomic Theory. New York: Macmillan, 1961.

Committee on Education and Labor, House of Representatives. Poverty in the United States. Washington: Government Printing Office, 1964.

Economic Report of the President and Annual Report of the Council of Economic Advisers, 1965. Washington: Government Printing Office, 1965.

SCHELLING; THOMAS C. National Income Behavior: An Introduction to Algebraic Analysis. New York: McGraw-Hill, 1951.

SCHULTZ, CHARLES L. National Income Analysis. Englewood Cliffs, N.J.: Prentice-Hall, 1964.

SIMLER, N. J. "The Structural Hypothesis and Public Policy," American Economic Review, December 1964.

---

[5]Economic Opportunity Act of 1964: Hearings Before the Subcommittee on the War on Poverty Program of the Committee on Education and Labor, House of Representatives, 88th Congress, 2d Session (Washington: Government Printing Office, 1964), pp. 26–30.

Chapter Six: THE ECONOMIC BENEFITS OF EDUCATION

THE GENERAL NATURE OF EDUCATIONAL RETURNS

In the United States, a vast army of teachers together with large numbers of auxiliary personnel have been engaged to work in educational establishments. Their salaries plus expenditures on materials, buildings, and the like represented an outlay of more than $39 billion in 1965–66. "This sum is second in size only to the national defense budget and there are many who think in a few years it will surpass even that expenditure, now running at about $49 billion."[1] For elementary and secondary schools alone, annual expenditures are now approaching $25 billion.

What outcome or "products" do we get from such large expenditures on educational establishments? Many people would say that "education" is provided for all willing students and let the matter go at that. Even quantitatively

---

[1]Richard Rutter, New York Times, Sept. 5, 1965, Section 3F, p. 1.

minded economists are inclined to ascribe paramount significance to the role of education in strengthening our democracy, in helping develop our cultural life, and in encouraging us to live our lives as decent human beings.

But economists have also become interested in classifying and analyzing the "economic benefits" of education; this, after all, is what their system of thought encourages them to do. To a degree their interest is theoretical and academic; even so, the studies of the contribution of education to the growth of our production system have recognized the school system as a major instrument of national policy.

In a sense, the development of work skills (although this is not the only thing that schooling accomplishes) is similar to the production of physical capital goods. "Both require the use over a period of time of facilities such as buildings, materials and equipment, and labor skills. Both necessitate the sacrifice of goods and services that might otherwise have been produced. Both will yield 'services' over some subsequent period."[2]

But the development of natural resources is really more analogous to education than the production of capital goods is. Natural resources, such as oil deposits, must be searched for and discovered; so must human talent. Indeed, the process of discovery should be one of the most absorbing tasks of the educational enterprise, and it must be said that neither the range nor the extent of human talents has yet been well explored. Like oil fields and agricultural land, human talent flourishes and subsequent yields are high when developmental efforts (or investments) are relatively great. Children who receive high-quality schooling today become the parents who provide a home environment that fosters receptivity to schooling in their children.

At the same time we must recognize that human talent has certain unique features when viewed as a natural resource. Physical resources that lie undiscovered or undeveloped ordinarily impose no maintenance costs on a society, but human beings do. Instead of offering a positive contribution to the life of an industrial country, the uneducated person is likely to impose net costs on the country, either for his living expenses (through welfare programs) or for the protection of other people from his antisocial acts (through police services, courts, and custody). Finally, human talent is unique among natural resources because its development provides the base for the discovery of new technology, under which the development of all resources, generally speaking, can become more effective.

---

[2] Richard S. Eckaus, "Education and Economic Growth," in *Economics of Higher Education*, ed. Selma Mushkin (Washington: Government Printing Office. 1962), p. 103.

INDIVIDUAL RETURNS FROM EDUCATION

A number of benefits of education can be said to accrue to the individual who receives the schooling. One of these is the opportunity to make a higher income. In 1963 the median income of male high school graduates was $6000, while those who had one to three years of high school earned $5153 on the average, and elementary school graduates received $4076.[3] But this is not all. Each time a person passes a certain level of education he acquires an "option" to pursue additional schooling and reap the additional benefits of that higher level.[4] Generally speaking, a person cannot attend college unless he has been graduated from high school. Therefore high school graduation has an economic value on two counts: it offers the chance to obtain a higher-paying job than those offered to dropouts, and it offers the option to continue one's education in college. Moreover, the more education a person obtains, the greater his range of job opportunities and the greater his security against unemployment. Education is a hedge against the personal economic vicissitudes of technological change. In the main, it is the better-educated worker on whom private employers will lavish on-the-job training. This is true for training made available in the person's first jobs and for the retraining offered him later, as well.[5]

FAMILY AND NEIGHBORHOOD BENEFITS OF EDUCATION

It is by no means true that all the benefits of schooling accrue to the individual who receives it. Some of the benefits most properly accrue to families and neighborhoods. One family benefit is that large numbers of mothers of young children enrolled in elementary schools are free to enter the labor force. There are about four million working mothers in the country, and their contribution to the national income is substantial, though whether this is a good thing for their children is not clear. (On the other hand, however, if fewer young children were actually enrolled in elementary school, the demand for elementary school teachers, which is one of the major employments for working mothers, would be reduced.) Another family benefit is the opportunity that members of educated families have to share cultural pleasures

---

[3]Council of Economic Advisers, *Annual Report* (Washington: Government Printing Office, 1965), p. 157.

[4]Burton A. Weisbrod, "Education and Investment in Human Capital," *Journal of Political Economy*, Supplement, October 1962, pp. 112–14.

[5]Jacob Mincer has estimated that in 1958 the on-the-job training costs for a person with an elementary education only were 28 percent of the cost for a person who had gone to college; that is, the less educated person had about a quarter as much further investment made in him after he went to work as was invested in the man with greater schooling. See "On-the-Job Training: Costs, Returns, and Some Implications," *Journal of Political Economy*, Supplement, October 1962.

in the home. Also, we should not ignore the fact that education is "produced" in the home. Children appear to learn a great deal from their parents; this is indicated by the difference in performance between children who come from homes of well-educated parents and those who come from homes where the parents have a minimum level of schooling. Not surprisingly, it turns out that approximately 40 percent of the variation among school districts in standard achievement test scores of elementary pupils is accounted for by the one variable of the educational level of adults in the district.[6] Investment in the education of one generation establishes a base from which a given volume of schooling for succeeding generations can provide a more extended development of intellectual skills.

What of neighborhood benefits? Whether or not members of neighborhoods engage in cultural activities together—and some clearly do not in the conventional sense—the adults of any section of a town gain returns because the children are in school many hours of the year and not wandering the streets subject to the temptations of vandalism and other such outlets for youthful energy. More practically, the social values inculcated in the schools ease the inevitable conflicts between the different generations.

BENEFITS TO THE EMPLOYER

Schooling has effects which profit individual business firms in various ways. Some firms have a strong commitment to on-the-job training for the development of craft, technical, engineering, and scientific skills of the members of their work forces. These firms are likely to be those that operate in the forefront of technology, providing the government with its instruments for defense and space exploration, and providing American industry with the tools of automated production. For these firms the pace of technological change is so rapid that the worker cannot be trained for specific new skills in technical schools or universities; instead, reliance must be placed on training efforts on the job. The quality of such training programs is quite probably a function of the quality of the trainees' previous schooling, because learning is in part a sequential process, and because it would seem that study habits developed in school carry over to the workplace. It is also very important to note that the quality of industrial training programs is related to the knowledge and skill of the *trainers*. Often the men who conduct the various kinds of formal and informal training sessions in industry are regular workers, not specially hired teachers. The ability of these men to impart their skills to the

---

[6]This and similar findings are presented in a report by Charles S. Benson, *State-Local Fiscal Cooperation in Education in California* (Sacramento, Calif.: Senate Fact-Finding Committee on Revenue and Taxation, 1965).

young is related, one would think, to the quality of their own schooling. If that schooling was of high quality, it should follow that the experienced workers in key industries would be able to keep abreast of the new developments in their fields and have sufficient confidence in their knowledge to be good instructors of younger workers.

All firms, whether or not they are on the forefront of technology, benefit from having an alert work force with stable work habits whose members can quickly grasp oral and written communications. Even though certain jobs such as punch press tending and assembly line work are not complicated in themselves, the relations between employers and employees regarding rates of pay, fringe benefits, social security arrangements, and arbitration proceedings become increasingly involved as our economy matures. Unless an efficient basis for communication exists, the morale of the work force will suffer and productivity will decline. Businessmen profess the belief that the schools can play an important role in developing a work force with this capacity. Lastly, all firms are likely to make use of the schools for personnel screening. For instance, it has been said that "many employers prefer or hire only college graduates, not because the particular jobs require any qualification to which a college education contributes anything, but only because a college degree serves them as a credential for the diligence and intelligence of the applicant."[7]

BENEFITS TO SOCIETY IN GENERAL

The categories of educational benefits we have listed so far do not exhaust the total yield. Education offers returns to the whole society, returns which are distributed more or less equally among its members. (These benefits correspond to the class of "social benefits" discussed in Chapter 4, which is to say that education, in part, is a collective good.) What, then, are the social benefits of education?

(1) All persons benefit from the discoveries of great scientists, and we are fortunate to live at a time when important discoveries are being made in medicine, agriculture, communications, and transportation. By and large, the modern scientist and inventor is a person of advanced education and training. It is reasonable to say that there is a relation between the quality of educational services a nation provides for its citizens and the rate of inventive activity in that society.

---

[7]Fritz Machlup, *The Production and Distribution of Knowledge in the United States* (Princeton, N.J.: Princeton Univ. Press, 1962), pp. 114–15. On the topic of employer-related benefits of schooling, see also Charles S. Benson and Paul R. Lohnes, "Skill Requirements and Industrial Training in Durable Goods Manufacturing," *Industrial and Labor Relations Review*, July 1959.

(2) All persons are likely to benefit from those increases in productivity that are engendered by education. This argument requires a somewhat extended treatment. We have noted that there is a positive relation between level of education and income (this topic will also be discussed in Chapter 8). While this relation has been explored rather carefully by economists and sociologists, it has not yet been possible to "disaggregate" the higher incomes of people with larger amounts of schooling into components that show how much of the extra income is attributable to education per se and how much is attributable to health, intelligence, family background, institutional wage rigidities, or other factors. That is, we do not yet know precisely how much education contributes to the rise in productivity, or how much of that rise in productivity is captured in the wages and salaries of people who possess the education or in the profits of people who employ them. But we can always make some assumptions. Let us assume that a substantial part of the higher incomes associated with education, say not less than 50 percent, reflects productivity increases that are attributable to education. After all, this simply implies that if person A has more years of schooling than person B, then A is likely to have acquired a more economically useful set of skills than B, and that he acquired them by staying in school longer. Now, let us make an unreasonable assumption. Suppose that all of the extra productivity attributable to education is taken in the form of higher wages, salaries, and profits, with the result that none of it is passed along to the consumers in the form of price reductions by the producing firms. Are there then any social benefits from education? The answer, even under this "unreasonable" assumption, remains yes. As long as we have government, we will be provided with public services, and taxes will be levied on us to finance them. Any rise in the level of income in the society reduces the tax rates required to finance the services (or more public services can be provided at the same tax rates). The reduction in rates applies to the uneducated as well as the educated.

(3) It appears that people brought up in a democratic society want to continue to live in such a society. But democracy implies literacy, and beyond literacy, it implies the capacity to understand the broad issues of policy at the federal, state, and local levels of government. For most people the ability to read is acquired in school, and in school they practice discussing issues of social policy. Schools, then, are instruments required for the effective working of the democratic state. Furthermore, it is likely that most people prefer to live in a society where social mobility is possible. In a democratic society, the chief instrument for providing whatever social mobility exists is the schools.

(4) Much of the pleasure one can take in education is, perforce, shared pleasure. "The possibility of conversing intelligently about subjects compre-

hensible only to the educated, and the sharing of experiences in art, music, and literature, are enjoyments which go beyond the satisfaction of the individual former student. Moreover, certain cultural services can be produced economically only for large audiences, so that many good books, good plays, operas, and concerts become available only if the number of those educated to appreciate them is large."[8] Thus there are social benefits of a cultural nature which all interested persons share in more or less equal measure.

EDUCATION AND LEISURE

As we move into a period where the workweeks are shorter, vacations longer, and sabbatical years (full-year leaves with pay) for mature workers a common feature of our social life, the fortunate man will be the one who is eager to use his free time in ways that mean something to him. It is likely that for most of us the skill requirements of leisure will exceed those of work for several reasons. First, there must be some intellectual basis for any interesting and absorbing use of large amounts of leisure time. People do not take pleasure in repeating the same actions over and over again; repetition is a characteristic of work, not leisure. Second, unlike the modern system of work, leisure activities are usually independent. At work, complicated tasks are often divided among several persons, and no one of them has to be able to understand the whole process. This is called division of labor, and it is one of the chief features of our highly productive industrial life. On the other hand, one of the chief pleasures of leisure is seeing things whole—understanding the whole operation—whether it is building shortwave radio sets, tying flies for fishing, painting pictures, or climbing mountains. Third, because of the nature of work in the modern day, a common standard is usually set for all the workers. But during his leisure time every man is his own boss, and one of his real pleasures is in surpassing whatever he has accomplished before. There is no common standard, and a man merely tries to improve on his past performance.

The one supreme gift a person can receive is time—time to use as he sees fit. Our children will probably be as bountifully supplied with time as we are with material goods. The education they are receiving today will largely determine whether they are successful in their use of these ever increasing amounts of time—whether, indeed, they receive this supreme gift eagerly or with boredom and indifference. Hopefully, they will recognize the opportunities for self-fulfillment that this gift offers.

Just as the concentration in our individual lives will shift from work to the enjoyment of leisure, the concentration in our national life may well shift

---

[8]Machlup, op. cit., p. 116.

from the production of automobiles, missiles, and the like to a concern with the arts. In the long view of history our country will be judged not just on the riches we amass or the power we hold, but on whether we create works of art that endure.

Although we may become as rich in leisure as we are in goods, there is absolutely no danger that our educational system will become obsolete. On the contrary, the demands placed upon it will grow. Our educational system today should help people enter the world of work, but this same system can provide the basis for developing the skills we will need for the greater leisure we will have.

IS EDUCATION CONSUMPTION OR INVESTMENT?

At various times economists have classified parts of education as a consumption good and other parts as investment. The general procedure has been to try to estimate what share of educational expenditures leads to increases in the earning power of individuals and what share leads only to personal enjoyment in reading, other cultural activities, and sports. This is a difficult kind of allocation to make. Instruction in art received by a nonprofessional may clearly be a consumers' good (although if it helps a man to be happy in his work, there is an element of the producers' good), and instruction in machine maintenance for a factory worker may clearly be a producers' good, but learning to read is surely both at the same time. The physician may have an aesthetic reaction to his work in biology, and the physicist to his study of mathematics.

The practical solution to the problem of dividing educational expenditures between consumption and investment is through recourse to rules of thumb, such as stating that all of elementary education, half of secondary, and all of higher education are investments. But a better approach may be the use of the criterion of time — the length of time during which educational benefits are received. The pleasure one takes in going to school and the immediate joy of learning would be considered consumption, but the use of education in cultural pursuits, extending as it does over a whole lifetime, would be regarded as investment. This approach has the advantage of conceptual simplicity, although we must admit that it is not readily applicable to allocating portions of school budgets between investment and consumption categories. At this time the difficulties involved in making these allocations appear to be insurmountable.

We have considered here some of the economic benefits of education. In Chapter 7 we shall turn to an examination of the various kinds of costs that are incurred in maintaining educational establishments. Then in Chapter 8 we shall review some of the recent efforts that economists have made to express in quantitative terms what educational benefits we receive in return for these costs.

Suggested Readings

Bowen, William G. *Economic Aspects of Education.* Princeton, N.J.: Industrial Relations Section, 1964.

Bowman, Mary Jean. "Human Capital: Concepts and Measures," in Salem J. Mushkin, *Economics of Higher Education.* Washington: Government Printing Office, 1962.

Daniere, Andre. *Higher Education in the American Economy.* New York: Random House, 1964.

Morgan, James N., and others. *Income and Welfare in the United States.* New York: McGraw-Hill, 1962.

Thomas, Lawrence. *The Occupational Structure and Education.* Englewood Cliffs, N.J.: Prentice-Hall, 1956.

Weisbrod, Burton A. *External Benefits of Education.* Princeton, N.J.: Industrial Relations Section, 1964.

Chapter Seven: THE COSTS OF EDUCATIONAL SERVICES

THE KNOWLEDGE INDUSTRY

In his recent volume *The Production and Distribution of Knowledge*, Fritz Machlup defines knowledge as "anything that is known by somebody" and the production of knowledge as "any activity by which someone learns of something *he* has not known before even if others have."[1] Machlup goes on to classify and discuss many branches of the "knowledge industry," branches as diverse as basic research in the physical sciences, the publication of newspapers and magazines, and the holding of religious conventions. We are concerned in this chapter with the "production costs" in one branch of the knowledge industry, education, and especially with costs of elementary and secondary schooling. Quantitatively speaking, education is the largest branch

---

[1]Fritz Machlup, *The Production and Distribution of Knowledge* (Princeton, N.J.: Princeton Univ. Press, 1962) p. 7.

of the knowledge industry, and the elementary and secondary schools are the largest component (in terms of cost) of the whole set of educational services.[2]

THE PEOPLE INVOLVED

In considering the cost of an economic activity, a good starting point is to note how many people are productively involved in that activity. Table V gives figures for a recent year on the demands that the elementary and secondary schools make on the human resources of the economy. The 44 million people who had an official or legal connection with the schools in 1959–60 represented 24.6 percent of the population—roughly one-quarter—and even so we must admit that the figures in Table I understate slightly the number of persons: no figures are available to show the numbers of noninstructional and administrative personnel in the nonpublic schools; also, no figures are available to show how many federal employees have full- or part-time responsibilities in administering programs that affect the elementary and secondary schools. But education is clearly our largest industry.

TABLE V

NUMBERS OF PERSONS ENGAGED FULL- OR PART-TIME
IN ELEMENTARY AND SECONDARY SCHOOL ACTIVITIES, 1955–60

Categories of Persons		Number
Public Schools		
Teachers		1,354,958
Other instructional personnel		109,073
Local administrative staff		18,747
Other local school employees		512,973
Full-time	441,919	
Part-time	71,054	
Local school board members, part-time		178,571
State administrative staff		10,640
State school board members, part-time		836
Pupils enrolled		36,086,771
Private Schools		
Instructional staff		175,633
Pupils enrolled		5,674,943
	TOTAL	44,123,145

SOURCE: U.S. Department of Health, Education, and Welfare, Office of Education, *Statistics of State School Systems, 1959–60* (Washington: Government Printing Office, 1963), pp. 21–37.

---

[2]For the year 1958 Machlup (*ibid.*, pp. 354–57) shows total costs of knowledge production to be $136.4 billion, of which $60.2 billion (or 44.1 percent) is accounted for by education. See below, pp. 75-76.

You may question why we saw fit to include pupils in Table V. By Machlup's definition of the "production of knowledge," obviously pupils should be counted, because they are engaged in learning something. But matters of strict definition aside, one can say that learning is a cooperative endeavor: during the school day, pupils expand their own powers of knowing but they also contribute to the knowledge of their classmates and, indeed, to the knowledge of their teachers.[3] Finally, the hours when children are in school or are engaged in doing homework are hours when the pupils could be doing work in the conventional sense. All countries have known child labor at one time or another, and the fact that we in the United States have come to rely less and less on the work of children is a matter of social convention, not of change in the biological characteristics of youth. School enrollment, then, represents what the economist calls "opportunity cost." Because children are in school, our society forgoes for the time being the opportunity to have the goods and services that those children could be producing if they were placed in factories, shops, and the like. From the social point of view, this cost is incurred in part for compassionate reasons and in part to reap the benefits of the "investment in man," as noted in the preceding chapter.[4]

Another index of the magnitude of public education is that it represents approximately 25 percent of total public employment. It is by far the single largest type of public service. In 1963 the number of positions in public education, including higher education, had reached a point where it exceeded *total federal employment* (excluding the armed services) by over 1 million persons.[5]

COSTS AS CONVENTIONALLY REPORTED

Table VI shows the cash outlay, classified by object or purpose of expenditure, of all public school districts in 1959–60. A few comments about the table are in order, even though many of the items included in it are self-explanatory. The largest single category of expenditure is instructional salaries

---

[3]Of course attitude is important. In service industries generally, the formal recipient of a service gains more of it if he seeks to cooperate with the practitioner than if he does not. This is true in the purchases of legal services and medical services as well as in education. It is conceivable that some children have such a negative attitude toward learning that they exert a deleterious influence on the acquisition of knowledge by their classmates, but these instances can probably be regarded as special cases.

[4]It is now common practice among economists to include an estimate of "forgone earnings" of secondary students (but not of elementary pupils) in their calculations of the costs of education, as we will see below.

[5]The figures are as follows: federal civilian employment in 1963, 1,772,000; employment in state and local (public) educational institutions, 2,886,000. U.S. Department of Commerce, Office of Business Economics, *Survey of Current Business*, July 1964, Table 52, p. 29.

(49.1 percent), but this by no means represents the total of salary payments of school districts. School employees' salaries are actually included in every item shown in the table except fixed charges (mainly contributions to employees retirement systems), capital outlay, and interest. It is not uncommon to find that salaries represent 80 percent of expenditures in individual school districts.

A corollary is that relatively little expenditure is made in public education on materials and tools to help the teacher carry out the processes of instruction. Note that only 4.4 percent of dollar outlays are found under "other instructional expenditures," but this heading includes supplies (paper, chalk, paints, and the like), library books, textbooks, and salaries of secretarial and clerical assistants to instructional personnel. It might be thought that massive purchases of instructional equipment are included under the rather large item, capital outlay (17.7 percent of total expenditures).[6] However, in the opinion

TABLE VI

LOCAL SCHOOL EXPENDITURES, 1959–60

Object or Function	Dollars (Thousands)	Percentage Share
Administration	528,408	3.4
Instructional salaries	7,671,250	49.1
Other instructional expenditures	679,487	4.4
Plant operation	1,085,036	6.9
Plant maintenance	422,586	2.8
Attendance services	27,948	0.2
Health services	100,993	0.6
Transportation services	486,338	3.1
Food services	372,975	2.4
Miscellaneous school services	45,042	0.3
Community services	57,953	0.4
Summer schools	13,263	0.1
Adult education	26,858	0.2
Community colleges	34,492	0.2
Fixed charges	909,323	5.8
Capital outlay	2,661,786	17.0
Interest	489,514	3.2
Total	15,613,252	100.0

SOURCE: U.S. Department of Health, Education, and Welfare, Office of Education, *Statistics of State School Systems, 1959–60* (Washington: Government Printing Office, 1963), pp. 57–73.

---

[6]Table VI relates to expenditures, not sources of funds. Most of what is reported in capital outlay does not fall in local tax resources in the year in which the outlay is incurred; rather, the money to finance the construction of school buildings and other projects is borrowed on long-term, and the debt is retired gradually over a 20- or 30-year period.

of a careful observer, Harold D. Clark of Columbia University, this is simply not so. Most capital outlay is for acquiring building sites, financing the construction of new schoolhouses, and remodeling old facilities — but not for instructional equipment. In 1890 the average school district spent well over 90 percent of its capital outlay on its buildings and something less than 10 percent on equipment. Professor Clark contends that about the same proportion of capital outlay continues to go for buildings today, even though in other types of economic activities there has been a shift toward relatively less expenditure on the building shell and more expenditure on the equipment.[7] In manufacturing, for example, about 75 percent of capital outlay is for equipment and only 25 percent is for factory building and sites. Education remains a peculiarly labor-intensive process, that is, it continues to rely to an extreme degree on human services as distinct from machine services.

THE DYNAMICS OF COST CHANGE

As Fig. 6 indicates, expenditures for elementary and secondary schools have increased handsomely in the last forty years. (The chart is drawn in a special way so that equal vertical distances represent equal percentage changes in the magnitudes illustrated.) All variables in Fig. 6 are in "real" terms, that is, in dollar values without the influence of general price change or inflation. It shows that instructional salaries, current expenditures per pupil (without capital outlay and interest charges), and total expenditure per pupil have advanced at a greater rate than national income per capita.

On the face of it, this is a startling fact. Public schools are tax-supported and no one is happy to pay more taxes. Educational policy in the United States is decentralized, so the expenditure increases have to be voted by local electorates. And, furthermore, the mainstay of local school support is the property tax, a relatively unpopular levy in which year-to-year increases are painfully visible.[8]

What, then, was the dynamic element in the rise in school costs? The complexity of judging what has been in the minds of voters in 40,000 school districts renders a final answer to this question elusive, but we can make a good guess: the dynamic element has been teachers' salaries.

Certain facts are consistent with this view. Between 1919–20 and 1959–60, 61.4 percent of this rise in direct expenditures for schools in real terms was represented by increases in the sums paid to teachers. The average level of

---

[7]Professor Clark's findings are reported in Jesse Burkhead, *Public School Finance* (Syracuse, N.Y.: Syracuse Univ. Press, 1964), p. 80.

[8]On the other hand, the sales tax, for example, is collected so gradually and painlessly that hardly anyone knows just how much he is paying.

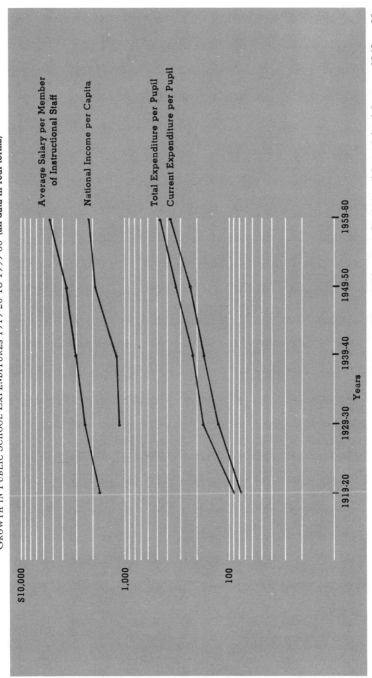

FIG. 6

GROWTH IN PUBLIC SCHOOL EXPENDITURES 1919-20 TO 1959-60 (all data in real terms)

Source: Office of Education, Statistics of State School Systems, 1963, p. 22.

teachers' salaries has been rising since 1950–51 at an annual rate of 7.5 percent, and this rate of advance is considerably in excess of the average gain in salaries and wages of all employed persons in the economy: 3.8 percent. In addition, it is increasingly the practice in school systems to figure administrative salaries, supervisory salaries, and (to a lesser extent) nonprofessional salaries on the basis of the classroom teachers' salary schedules.

But what is the force behind the upward movement in teachers' salaries? We must recognize, after all, that teachers' organizations have only recently obtained the right of collective bargaining, and even now they have it in only a few states. However, practically all teachers are paid under a "single salary schedule," with the pay of any individual teacher in a school district determined basically by two factors: seniority and extent of formal training. Furthermore, the teaching profession is characterized by a high rate of turnover, that is, voluntary resignation from service in a particular district. Therefore, even aside from the hiring necessary because of pupil enrollment, a typical district enters the market every spring to hire about ten teachers for every hundred in its employ.[9] In the short run, the one important variable a school district can manipulate to improve its competitive position in the market for teachers' services is its salary schedule. Finally, it has come to be accepted that a school district should not pay a higher salary to its newly hired teachers (taking into account experience and training) than it pays to those who continue in its service. Therefore the single salary schedule is itself a kind of automatic instrument of collective bargaining, which, given the existence of a high rate of turnover, cannot fail to be effective in raising the average level of teachers' pay and, hence, the rate of spending on the school services.[10]

THE AGGREGATE OF EDUCATIONAL COSTS: PROFESSOR MACHLUP'S ESTIMATES

As we noted at the beginning of this chapter, Professor Machlup has taken an inclusive view of the nature of education and of the "knowledge industry" generally. He has assembled cost estimates for education that are similarly broad, and to gain perspective on the commitment of the United

---

[9]Ward S. Mason, The Beginning Teacher, Status and Career Orientation (Washington: Government Printing Office, 1961), p. 95.

[10]Parents, of course, are concerned about the quality of teachers hired in the district in which they live. Should a district lag behind its rivals in recruitment salaries, it would find it necessary to make quite a large jump in local tax levy to restore its competitive position. Large increases in local tax levies are often difficult to obtain. It is thus incumbent on a superintendent to urge a policy that matches (or overmatches) the salary increases of neighboring districts; otherwise he courts a deteriorating situation that may become extremely difficult to correct.

States to educational processes it is instructive to see what these estimates reveal. (Because of difficulties of bringing masses of data together, the estimates are available only for the years 1955–56 and 1957–58.) Table VII reproduces the Machlup figures on the total costs of education.

There are several important differences between the Machlup estimates and cost figures as they are conventionally reported. Educational services offered by business firms (training on the job), churches, the armed services, and proprietary institutions are included in the list. Income forgone by mothers in the home, by high school students, and by college students is taken into account. Estimates of the rental value of school properties are put in the list, as are estimates of the number of tax exemptions governments offer to nonprofit educational institutions.

For purposes of relating the costs of education to national product, Machlup suggests that the following magnitudes be used: GNP in 1955–56, $433,447 million; GNP in 1957–58, $468,192 million. Accordingly, the $51,172 million of education costs in 1955–56 represented 11.8 percent of GNP and the $60,194 million of educational cost in 1957–58 accounted for 12.9 percent of GNP. It can only be concluded that the investment in education in the United States is of formidable size.

TABLE VII

TOTAL COST OF EDUCATION, 1955–56 AND 1957–58 (MILLIONS OF DOLLARS)

	1955-56	1957-58
Education in the Home		
Income forgone by mothers staying home to educate their preschool children	4,341	4,432
Training on the Job		
Formal training programs operated by firms	800	1,000
Production loss and cost of training newly hired workers	1,940	2,054
TOTAL	2,740	3,054
Education in the Church		
Current congregational expenses	1,400	1,588
New construction of churches and synagogues	775	879
TOTAL	2,175	2,467
Education in the Armed Services		
Expenditures for special training schools and programs (including trainees' maintenance)	1,100	1,100
Expenditure for basic training	1,810	1,810
Cash payments to military special trainees	500	500
TOTAL	3,410	3,410

TABLE VII (Cont.)

	1955–56	1957–58
Elementary and Secondary Education		
Current expenditures, public schools	8,568	10,716
Current expenditures, nonpublic schools	1,295	1,642
Plant expansion, public schools	2,387	2,853
Plant expansion, nonpublic schools	361	437
Implicit rent, public schools	1,912	2,392
Implicit rent, nonpublic schools	288	352
Cost of tax exemptions, public schools	800	890
Cost of tax exemptions, nonpublic schools	120	132
Earnings forgone by high school students	11,211	13,519
Transportation, supplies, and clothing	336	406
TOTAL	27,278	33,339
Higher Education		
Current allowable expenditures, public institutions	1,324	1,712
Current allowable expenditures, nonpublic institutions	959	1,188
Plant expansion, public institutions	416	711
Plant expansion, nonpublic institutions	270	411
Implicit rent, nonpublic institutions	313	344
Cost of tax exemptions, public institutions	172	181
Cost of tax exemptions, nonpublic institutions	130	136
Earnings forgone by college and university students	6,139	7,024
Earnings forgone by medical interns and residents	144	165
Transportation, supplies, and clothing	368	421
TOTAL	10,634	12,757
Commercial Vocational and Residential Special Schools		
Gross "sales" of commercial vocational schools	196	223
Current costs of residential special schools	23	30
TOTAL	219	253
Federal Funds for Education		
Funds not elsewhere included (various training programs and the like)	241	342
Public Libraries		
Operating expenses	122	140
Capital outlay	12	n.a.
TOTAL	134	140
GRAND TOTAL	$ 51,172	$ 60,194

---

[1]SOURCE: Fritz Machlup, *The Production and Distribution of Knowledge in the United States* (Princeton, N.J.: Princeton Univ. Press, 1962), pp. 104–5.

Suggested Readings

BECKER, GARY S. *Human Capital: A Theoretical Analysis.* New York: Columbia Univ. Press, 1965.

BLITZ, RUDOLPH C. "The Nation's Educational Outlay," in SELMA J. MUSHKIN, *Economics of Higher Education.* Washington: Government Printing Office, 1962.

MACHLUP, FRITZ. *The Production and Distribution of Knowledge.* Princeton, N.J.: Princeton Univ. Press, 1962.

National Education Association. *Financing the Public Schools, 1960–1970.* Washington: the Association, 1962.

U.S. Department of Health, Education, and Welfare, Office of Education. *Statistics of State School Systems, 1959–60.* Washington: Government Printing Office, 1963.

VAIZEY, JOHN. *The Costs of Education.* London: Allen & Unwin, 1958.

Chapter Eight: QUANTITATIVE MEASUREMENT OF EDUCATIONAL BENEFITS

SOME SIGNIFICANT QUESTIONS

When farm people move to the cities and take nonfarm jobs, it commonly happens that they earn less money than urban-born workers. When Negro workers move from the South to take jobs in Eastern cities, they frequently earn less than their white peers. When an older worker is displaced from his job, he is likely to have greater difficulty in finding a new one than the younger worker does. These differences may be attributed to sociological factors or to blind prejudice, but the true cause may be differences in the quantity or quality of their education.

Why, in the face of the extreme devastation of physical capital in Europe during World War II, were the ravaged countries able to reestablish their prewar standards of living so quickly? The answer may be that their human capital, as represented by the stock of education in their surviving population, was relatively untouched. Why, in the face of crying needs for economic development in the poor countries of the world, is their ability to absorb increments of physical capital so limited? The answer may be that their stock of human capital, required as a complement to the effective deployment of physical means of production, is miserably undeveloped. Why has the volume of production in the United States advanced at a greater pace than can be explained by taking account of changes in the physical volume of capital and man-hours worked? The answer may be that we are receiving returns from past investments in the education of the population. Questions and speculations like these have led economists to seek quantitative measurements of the yield of expenditures on education.[1] In this chapter we will consider the techniques of measurement — and also some implications of those measurements — as developed by three authorities: Herman P. Miller, Theodore W. Schultz, and Edward F. Denison.

THE PRIVATE RETURNS: HERMAN P. MILLER

In studying private returns to education, it is common practice to make extensive use of data on the income of households and employed individuals that is normally collected by the U.S. Bureau of the Census at ten-year intervals. The essential procedure is to see how incomes of households and individuals differ according to their levels of educational attainment. Do college graduates have, on the average, higher lifetime earnings than secondary school graduates? This is the sort of question one asks, and one looks for a systematic relation between education and income.

One of the most important analysts of census data is Herman P. Miller. Since 1956 he has been publishing his findings on the connection between income and education, and it is certainly fair to say that he is a pioneer in the field of the economics of education. He is fortunately placed to conduct such studies, because for some years he has carried heavy responsibilities in various technical capacities in the Bureau of the Census.

Before we look at some of the recent figures presented by Dr. Miller, we should note what it means to compute estimates of lifetime earnings. The process is sort of an actuarial, or life insurance, type of exercise. (1) Of a group of 100,000 male children (one could compute similar figures for females, if one wished, but the earnings of males and females are sufficiently different that the estimates of lifetime earnings for the two sexes should be prepared separately), survival tables tell us that about 96,000 will live to age 18. (2) Of the 96,000 who live to age 18, about 95,000 will survive to age 24. Between the ages of 18 and 24, this group of young men will live 666,000 man-years. From the 1960 census one determines the average earnings per year for men

---

[1]These and other questions are posed in Theodore W. Schultz, "Investment in Human Capital," *American Economic Review*, March 1961, pp. 3–7.

18 to 24 years old — the figure is approximately $2700. Our group of 18-to-24-year-olds, then, has earnings of about *$1.8 billion* (666,000 man-years × $2700). (3) Of the 95,000 who live to age 24, roughly 93,000 will survive to age 34. Between these ages they will have lived 938,000 man-years. For men 25 to 34, average earnings in 1960 were $5200 a year. The total expected earnings of men in this age bracket is *$4.9 billion* (938,000 × $5200). (4) The process is repeated through the higher age brackets, until we have exhausted the length of working life. Expected earnings for all age brackets are cast up — that is, we add the italicized figures above: $1.8 billion, $4.9 billion, and so on. For 1960 the total is $21.9 billion. This figure is then divided by 96,000 (the number of men who survive to the working age of 18) to find the average lifetime earnings figure of $229,000. This is what the typical U.S. male could expect to earn over his lifetime, if the wage and salary structure prevailing in 1960 would continue into the future.

It is entirely feasible to carry out this process for males who are different in their level of education.[2] Table VIII offers figures that show the sharp rise in lifetime earnings that is associated with higher levels of education. The difference in earnings of the college graduate and the high school graduate is $138,000.

TABLE VIII

LIFETIME EARNINGS OF MALES IN VARIOUS EDUCATIONAL GROUPS
(1960 Census Figures)

All Males (average)	$229,000
Elementary School	
Less than 8 years	143,000
8 years	184,000
High School	
1 to 3 years	212,000
4 years	247,000
College	
1 to 3 years	293,000
4 years	385,000
5 years or more	455,000

SOURCE: Herman P. Miller, *Rich Man, Poor Man* (New York: Thomas Y. Crowell, 1964), p. 148.

Back in 1930, college graduates were estimated to have lifetime earnings $35,000 greater than those of high school graduates. It is estimated that in

---

[2]Miller has recently suggested a new process of computing lifetime earnings which introduces the dynamic element of economic growth into the process. See his article "Lifetime Income and Economic Growth," *American Economic Review*, September 1965, pp. 834–44.

those days four years of college cost $6400 in total, counting tuition, room, board, and the like. The college graduate received, on the average, 5.5 times as much extra income as his college education cost him. Current college costs are a little more than double what they were in 1930; that is, about $14,500 for four years. But today the college graduate receives 9.5 times as much in extra income as college costs ($138,000 extra income divided by $14,500 costs)! College education has actually improved as an investment, even though the supply of college graduates has increased enormously since 1930.[3]

One other observation of Miller's should be noted here: that even for people in the same lines of work, education pays. The return is not strictly a matter of more education leading to different (and higher-paying) kinds of work. Table IX shows average 1960 earnings of white men, aged 35 to 44, in various occupations, differentiated by level of schooling completed. Clearly, education offers a handsome private return in the form of higher incomes.

TABLE IX

EARNINGS OF MALES IN SPECIFIED OCCUPATIONS, 1960, BY LEVEL OF SCHOOLING

	Less than High School Graduate	High School Graduate
Bricklayers	$5100	$6300
Carpenters	4800	5700
Electricians	6100	6600
Toolmakers	6700	7300
Bus drivers	4400	5400
Firemen	5300	6100

SOURCE: Herman P. Miller, *Rich Man, Poor Man* (New York, Thomas Y. Crowell, 1964), p. 145.

RETURNS FROM EDUCATIONAL STOCK: THEODORE W. SCHULTZ

Now let us go to yet another examination of costs and benefits of education — the work of Theodore W. Schultz in developing the concept of educational stocks. Professor Schultz begins his analysis by estimating the cost of education for various years since 1900. The procedure is involved, but essentially the steps are as follows:[4] From gross expenditures of educational

[3] The estimates for 1930 are to be found in J. W. Walsh, "Capital Concept Applied to Man," *Quarterly Journal of Economics*, February 1935, pp. 256 ff. Since one man's income is another man's price, we can say that the society is paying far too much for the services of college graduates — paying more, that is, for these services than it costs to "produce" them.

[4] The procedure is explained in detail in Theodore W. Schultz, "Capital Formation by Education," *Journal of Political Economy*, December 1960.

establishments, the sums spent on capital outlay and auxiliary enterprises are subtracted, yielding estimates of net expenditures. To net expenditures is added a value for interest and depreciation on physical property, and the sum represents "annual resource costs." (The figures for interest and depreciation represent how much physical capital is "used up" each year by educational establishments.) To the sum of resource costs is added a value for income forgone by high school and college students.[5] The sum of resource costs, income forgone, and "additional expenditures" (money spent on books, supplies, extra clothes, and privately financed travel to and from educational institutions) equals the total costs of education.[6] Total costs are converted to a per-student basis for the elementary, secondary, and college levels separately.

In preparing his estimates of the stock of educational capital, Schultz chose to use cost-per-pupil figures for the base year of 1956. In that year the cost figures were these: elementary, $280; high school, $1420; college and university, $3300. The main procedures in estimating stock are illustrated in Table X, referring to the year 1957.

TABLE X

Costs of Education in Labor Force in 1957 as Measured by Years of School per Member

	1	2	3
	Years of School per Member	Cost per Year in 1956 Prices	Cost per Member of Labor Force
Elementary	7.52	$ 280	$2106
High School	2.44	1420	3458
College and University	0.64	3300	2099
Total	10.60		$7663

Source: Theodore W. Schultz, "Education and Economic Growth," in *Social Forces Influencing American Education, 1961* (Chicago: National Society for the Study of Education), 1961, p. 70.

Column 1 of Table X indicates the average school years completed per member of the labor force. On the average, workers in 1957 had 7.52 years of elementary school, 2.44 years of high school, and 0.64 year of college. The cost

---

[5]For each relevant year, earnings forgone by high school students are estimated at 11 times the average weekly earnings of workers in manufacturing and at 25 times the average weely earnings for college and university students. The factors of 11 and 25 are intended to take account of the relation of starting wage to average wage and of unemployment.

[6]The "additional expenditures" are estimated to be 10 percent of forgone earnings.

figures in column 2 are explained in the preceding paragraph. Column 3 is the product of columns 1 and 2, and shows the cost per member at each level of education. The total stock of education per member of the work force in 1957 was $7663. The costs per member are then converted to average cost per school year: $7663 ÷ 10.6 = $723.

The next step is to compute the number of years of education possessed by members of the work force in 1957: the figure is 740 million. Multiplying this figure by the cost per year, $723, yields a total stock of $435 billion. A similar procedure is employed to compute stocks in other periods, and the results are shown in Table XI. For comparison, changes in the stock of non-human capital are also shown. Clearly, human capital has been increasing at a greater rate than nonhuman.

Table XI does not show the change in the total stock of education in the population, since it deals only with members of the labor force. This is the way Schultz chose to allocate the production of education between its investment (work force) and consumption (nonwork force) uses. The procedure removes about 37 percent of the stock of education from the investment category.

TABLE XI

Total Value of the Stock of Education and of Reproducible Nonhuman Wealth in the United States, 1900 to 1957, in 1955 or 1956 Prices

	Educational Stock of Labor Force 14 Years and Older	Stock of Reproducible Nonhuman Wealth
1900	63	282
1910	94	403
1920	127	526
1930	180	735
1940	248	756
1950	359	969
1957	535	1270

What contribution did the use of the stock of education make to national economic growth? Schultz approaches this question in the following manner: Taking the period 1929 to 1957, he notes that real national income in the United States rose from $150 billion to $302 billion, a gain of $152 billion. During the same time the stock of education in the labor force went up from $180 billion to $535 billion, a gain of $355 billion. The size of the labor force, however, rose by 38 percent; hence, to hold the stock of education per member of the labor force constant, the 1930 value of that stock, $180 billion (Table XI), had to be increased by 38 percent. Thirty-eight percent of $180 billion is $69 billion. Thus the net change in educational stock was $286 billion ($355 billion minus $69 billion). The only further problem is to estimate a rate of return on this net increase in educational stock.

Schultz suggests that it may be appropriate to use a rate of return of 11 percent, because, among other reasons, the ratio of the additional earnings of college graduates over those of high school graduates to the cost of college education had a value of approximately 11 in 1958. (The exact figures are as follows: extra earnings of college graduates, $151,000; cost of college, $13,780; ratio of returns to costs, 10.96.)[7]

Applying a rate of return of 11 percent to the $286 billion net investment in human capital gives a dollar yield of $31.5 billion. Between 1929 and 1957, then, the net increase in educational stock produced a rise in real national income of $31.5 billion, assuming a rate of return from education investment of 11 percent. This $31.5 billion represents approximately 21 percent of the rise in real national income between 1929 and 1957 (31.5 / 152 × 100).

EDUCATION AS A SOURCE OF ECONOMIC GROWTH: EDWARD F. DENISON

In a major study that he completed recently, Edward F. Denison of the Brookings Institution sought to investigate three major questions: what have been the sources of economic growth in the United States in the past; what rate of growth can be anticipated in the future if no special actions are taken to change the growth rate; and what would be the effect on the future growth rate of various actions that might be taken to change it?[8]

Dr. Denison assumes that it is possible to separate the two main types of educational contributions to economic growth: (a) raising of the quality (that is, productivity) of the labor force and (b) increasing the stock of knowledge itself. His method of treating the former contribution is the more interesting.

Denison derived for various years the distribution of male workers by the number of years of school they had completed. He also determined the number of days attendance represented by a year's schooling at these same points of time. Next he obtained income differentials by years of schooling among workers of the same age, using the census data for 1949. These differentials are shown in Table XII. At this point Denison introduced a key assumption: that 60 percent (but only 60 percent) of the observed differences in income by years of schooling are due to education, and the remainder are accounted for

---

[7] Schultz also applies alternative rates of return to the increase in educational stock, but this takes us beyond the reach of this short volume. See his "Education and Economic Growth," in Social Forces Influencing American Education 1961 (Chicago: National Society for the Study of Education, 1961), p. 81. A more technically refined method of estimating rates of returns from education is given in Gary S. Becker, Human Capital (New York: Columbia Univ. Press, 1964), Chap. 3.

[8] Edward F. Denison, The Sources of Economic Growth in the United States and the Alternatives Before Us (New York: Committee for Economic Development), 1962.

by differences in ability, by nepotism, and by a host of other factors. Column 2 of Table V shows the income differentials after they have been adjusted by two-fifths.

TABLE XII

INCOME DIFFERENTIALS BY YEARS OF EDUCATION, 1949, AVERAGE OF SELECTED AGE CLASSES OF MALES

	(1)	(2)
Years of School Completed	Mean Income as % of Mean Income of Eighth-Grade Graduates	Mean Income Differential Used to Represent Effect of Education (% of Income of Eighth-Grade Graduates)
None	50	70
Elementary School		
1–4 years	65	79
5–7 years	80	88
8 years	100	100
High School		
1–3 years	115	109
4 years	140	124
College		
1–3 years	165	139
4 years or more	235	181

SOURCE: Edward F. Denison, *The Sources of Economic Growth in the United States and the Alternatives Before Us* (New York: Committee for Economic Development, 1962), p. 69.

The differentials of column 2, Table XII, were applied to the actual 1949 earnings of eighth-grade graduates, and these dollar figures of earnings, distinguished by years of school completed, were used to compute how the income of the male labor force would have changed if the only variable at play had been changes in the distribution of the level of education in the work force. To illustrate, Denison had figures on the numbers of males in the work force in 1910 who had no formal schooling, 1 to 4 years of elementary school, 5 to 7 years of elementary school, and so on. Each worker with no formal schooling would be credited with a wage equal to 70 percent of the eighth-grade graduate's wage in 1949; those with 1 to 4 years of elementary school would be credited with 79 percent; those with 5 to 7 years, with 88 percent; and so on. The total of wages paid (hypothetically) in 1910 was added up and the average wage computed. The same process was repeated for 1920. The average wage computed for 1920 would be greater than that for 1910. Why? Only because the years of schooling possessed by the members of the work force had increased. The method allows one to isolate the effect of changes in the level of schooling, as counted in years, on average income.

This is not the whole story, however, because not only did the average number of years of schooling per member of the work force increase, but the school year lengthened also. Denison assumed that the increase in the number of days per years of schooling had the same effect on labor productivity that the increase in number of years did. The computational procedure computing the influence of the longer school year can be illustrated by the following figures:

1. Between 1930 and 1960, labor output per man, considering only years of schooling, increased by 12.8 percent.

2. In the same period the average number of years of school completed rose by 29.4 percent and the average number of days per school year by 34.8 percent. Multiplying these two figures together as indexes (129.4 × 134.8), we obtain a percentage increase in days of school per person: 73.7.

3. The ratio of days of school completed to years of school completed is 2.51 (73.7 ÷ 29.4).

4. The 12.8 percent rise in labor output through years of school only is multiplied by the factor of 2.51 to obtain 32.1 percent, which is the rise in labor output, taking account both of the increase in years and the greater number of school days per year. The average annual rise in labor productivity between 1930 and 1960 that is attributable to education is 1.1 percent (32.1 divided by 30 years).

Denison, like Schultz, is interested in discovering the share of economic growth that education accounts for, and he uses the same major base period, 1929–57. Denison estimates that between 1929 and 1957 the increase in quantity of education raised the average quality of labor at an annual rate of 0.93 percent. The average share of labor in national income (wages, salaries, fees, and the like) during this period was 73 percent. Taking 73 percent of 0.93 percent yields 0.68 percentage point per annum, which is the average annual contribution of education to economic growth, as reflected in improved labor skills.[9] The average growth rate of national income itself was 2.93 percentage points between 1929 and 1957. Thus education's share of growth was 23 percent (0.68 divided by 2.93), and this estimate is remarkably close to that obtained by Schultz (21 percent), who used a rather different method.

What of the future? Denison concludes that the prospects for raising the growth rate through the quantitative extension of educational services are quite limited:

---

[9] This process of multiplying the annual rise in labor productivity by labor's share of national income can be made clear with a simple arithmetic example. Suppose national income in a given year is $100 billion. Let labor income equal 75 percent, or $75 billion. If labor output (which equals income) goes up by 1 percent, 0.75 billion, the national income rises to $100.75 billion. National income therefore increased by three-quarters of 1 percent for a 1 percent rise in labor output.

"Suppose that, starting with those who would otherwise complete school in 1962 and continuing indefinitely, some action were taken that resulted in everyone remaining in school one year longer than he otherwise would. Suppose further, as would be in rough accord at prospective educational levels with the differentials [reproduced in Table V], that the additional year raised the ability of these individuals to contribute to production by 7.5 percent.

"By 1970 only about 15 percent of the labor force would have benefited by extra education, and the average quality of the entire labor force would therefore be raised by 1.1 percent. But loss of those in school instead of at work in 1970 would cost us about 2.6 percent of the labor force. If these young workers are counted as of half the quality of the average worker, this would mean an offsetting loss of 1.3 percent of labor output. On balance, total labor input, adjusted for quality, would be reduced by 0.2 percent . . .

"Ultimately, sometime around the year 2010, the quality of the entire labor force would be raised by 7.5 percent, while the cost in labor lost that year would still be around 1.3 percent. Labor input would be larger by 6.2 percent and national product by 5.2 percent. Over the entire 50-year period from 1960 to 2010 we should have raised the average annual growth of national product by 0.10 percentage points."

Even this gain has to be adjusted downward (to 0.09 percentage point a year) to offset the direct costs of running educational establishments — the costs, that is, of the extra teachers, and so on, necessary to provide everybody with one more year of schooling. The fairly modest return from a fairly substantial increase in educational provision has two bases of explanation. (1) It is only increases in educational provision that yield increases in national income. Any level of school provision once attained simply supports the status quo. This is so even though the effects of an increase in educational provision may take many years to work themselves out. (2) Any increases in the quantitative extension of educational services that we can now imagine are necessarily modest in comparison with what has been accomplished in the past. The average number of days a child spends in elementary and secondary school has doubled over what it was in 1870. We cannot expect to have another doubling by the year 2000 — think what this would mean in terms of length of school life!

However, one should not be gloomy. Gains in productivity will accrue to the economy as improvements in the quality of the educational services occur — quality as distinct from quantitative extension of services. Furthermore, Denison estimates that the "advance of knowledge," or technological improvement, has contributed 20 percent of the growth in national income between 1929 and 1957. This source of economic growth may rise in the future, and it is generally accepted that elementary and secondary school services contribute to the "advance of knowledge" even though the relationship is not clearly defined at this time.[10]

A SUMMARY NOTE

As Professor Bowen of Princeton University has pointed out, "the results obtained for the U.S. economy do offer rather consistent (some might say surprisingly consistent) support for the notion that education, on the average, has paid significant financial as well as nonfinancial rewards."[11] But no one would claim that the assessment of returns to education is yet a refined topic of investigation. The methods used to date rely heavily upon observed income differentials, but income differentials reflect natural ability as well as education. The task of separating these two factors remains illusive. (Denison, you will recall, arbitrarily chose a 60-40 split between education and other factors in the allocation of the differentials.) A second problem is the relation between education, earnings differentials, and productivity differentials. On-the-job training in a machine-tool plant ordinarily increases the capacity of an individual to do advanced types of work in that plant. As he receives more training and takes on the performance of more demanding tasks, his pay goes up. Here the connection between education and earnings differential and between earnings differentials and productivity is relatively straightforward and clear. These relations become much less clear when one thinks of the education received by students in general high school programs and liberal arts college programs. Employers, it appears, do pay higher wages, other things equal, to high school graduates than to those who dropped out, and they tend to pay higher salaries to college graduates than to high school graduates. Suppose a printing company adopts a policy that all its newly hired salesmen shall be college graduates. Is it necessarily true that these salesmen are more productive than the company's draftsmen who, let us say, completed high school only? Or, if they are, do their salary differentials measure the difference in productivity with accuracy? Finally, is there a relation between what the salesmen studied in college and their capacity to perform work for the printing company? These are some of the difficult questions that plague those who seek to measure returns from education in quantitative terms.

---

[10]The upper limit of the contribution of education to economic growth in Denison's calculations thus becomes 43 percent: 23 percent through improvement of quality of labor and 20 percent from "advance of knowledge," assuming that all the "advance of knowledge" component could properly be allocated to education.

[11]William G. Bowen, *Economic Aspects of Education* (Princeton, N.J.: Industrial Relations Section), 1964, p. 32.

Suggested Readings

BOWMAN, MARY JEAN. "Schultz, Denison, and the Contribution of 'Eds' to National Income Growth," Journal of Political Economy, October 1964.

DENISON, EDWARD F. The Sources of Economic Growth in the United States and the Alternatives Before Us. New York: Committee for Economic Development, 1962.

HANSEN, W. L. "Total and Private Rates of Return to Investment in Schooling," Journal of Political Economy, April 1963.

HIESTAND, DALE L. Economic Growth and Employment Opportunities for Minorities. New York: Columbia Univ. Press, 1964.

SCHULTZ, THEODORE W. "Education and Economic Growth," in Social Forces Influencing American Education 1961. (60th Yearbook of the National Society for the Study of Education.) Chicago: the Society, 1961.

VAIZEY, JOHN. The Economics of Education. London: Faber & Faber, 1962.

Chapter Nine: EDUCATIONAL PLANNING

THE RATIONALE OF PLANNING

Generally speaking, planning in any activity is evidence of rationality. Planning implies the specification of objectives, the evaluation of alternative means to achieve the stated objectives, and the preparation of a time schedule under which the objectives are to be fulfilled. Even the best-devised plans should not represent an iron mold from which no changes are allowed; rather, plans should be revised periodically as the target dates for the achievement of various subgoals are approached. This is simply another way of saying that the effectiveness of planning is a function of the quality of information made available to the responsible authorities, and information ordinarily improves the closer one gets to target dates. The effectiveness of the use of planning is a function of the cooperation offered by the groups involved in supplying some particular service.

In those English-speaking countries that are highly developed, educational planning is not wholly absent, but it has never been vigorously pursued. In England, for example, there has long been a concern with adjusting the number of "grammar school" places (grammar schools are secondary schools of an extremely academic type) to the estimated number of qualified applicants. Presently there is great interest in adjusting the number of university places upward to meet the rising tide of persons formally qualified to pursue university education.[1] In the postwar period considerable attention has been given to adjusting the supply of newly trained primary and secondary teachers to the demand for their services, though these efforts have not been wholly successful. With this exception, the government has not sought to regulate the general structure of the educational system or of departmental or course offerings to its economic demands. But. preparatory work to allow this to be done, if it should be judged desirable, is now under way.

In the United States there has been even less educational planning, but the situation is changing somewhat. A number of states, including such leaders in the field as California, Illinois, Michigan, and New York, are seriously engaged in the planning of higher education. These states attempt to provide a place in their universities for qualified secondary school students by estimating in advance how many will meet the entrance requirements. The same procedure is used for state colleges and junior or community colleges. There is not, however, any close adjustment of the size of professional schools or university and college departments, or of course offerings, to the future occupational requirements of the state or region.

On the other hand, the "package" of federal acts, including specifically the Area Redevelopment Act, the Manpower Training and Development Act, the Economic Opportunity Act, the Vocational Education Act of 1963, and the Higher Education Facilities Act, represent among them a scheme of national educational planning under which the changing occupational characteristics of the economy would be considered in regulating the course structure offered to postelementary students.[2] Emphasis is placed, of course, on programs taken by youths who do not intend to go to a four-year liberal arts college. It cannot truly be said that techniques for implementing the different federal acts or for obtaining coordination among the various groups involved in their implementation have been fully worked out, but it would be hard to deny that there is an upsurge of interest in educational planning in the United States. The same is true in England.

---

[1] In October 1963 Lord Robbins, a distinguished economist of the London School of Economics, and his committee presented their long-awaited report *Higher Education* (London, Her Majesty's Stationery Office, 1963), containing a general plan for the further development of all branches of higher education in Great Britain.

[2] Similarly, in Canada there has recently been considerable interest in a rationalization of manpower development, as in the Technical and Vocational Training Assistance Act, 1960. See Dean H. Goard, "Current Developments in Canadian Technical and Vocational Education," *Phi Delta Kappan*, April 1965, p. 395.

THE CONTEXT OF EDUCATIONAL PLANNING:
UNDERDEVELOPED COUNTRIES

It is in the underdeveloped countries, however, that one finds the greatest commitment to educational planning. Let us look first at the basis for their concern about planning; then we shall consider in broad outline the technique of developing a national educational plan.

Professors Harbison and Myers have recently developed a taxonomy of the countries of the world, under which nations are classified by their stage of development.[3] They used measures both of economic development per se and of human resource development. The indexes chosen to measure economic development were gross national product per capita, the percentage of the active population engaged in agriculture, public expenditures on education as a percentage of national income, and percentage of total population in the age group 5 to 14. In measuring human resource development, the variables included the number of teachers (primary and secondary) per 10,000 population, engineers and scientists per 10,000 population, physicians and dentists per 10,000 population, percentage of the population aged 4 to 14 that are enrolled in primary education, percentage of the population aged 15 to 19 enrolled in secondary education, percentage of the population aged 20 to 24 enrolled in higher education, percentage of students enrolled in scientific and technical faculties, and percentage of students enrolled in faculties of humanities, fine arts, and law.[4] The choice of variables was influenced, of course, by the kinds of data that are available for a very large number of countries.

Four categories of countries were established. The "advanced" group includes such nations as the United States, the U.S.S.R., the United Kingdom, Germany, Canada, France, the Scandinavian countries (except Norway), Australia, New Zealand, and Japan. You are familiar with the levels of income and educational attainment in these countries. Similarly, aside from differences in language and custom, you could feel at home in the next category, the "semiadvanced" nations. This group comprises Mexico, India, Spain, Greece, Italy, Chile, and Norway, among others. Our interest here is more particularly in the characteristics of the two lower groups, the "underdeveloped" countries and the "partially developed."

Underdeveloped countries comprise Ethiopia, Afghanistan, Saudi Arabia, the Congo, Nigeria, and Haiti, among others. Income in this group is very low, seldom rising as high as $150 per capita per year. Typically, over 70 percent of the population is engaged in agriculture (the average for the group

---

[3]Frederick Harbison and Charles A. Myers, *Education, Manpower and Economic Growth* (New York: McGraw-Hill, 1964).
[4]*Ibid.*, p. 27.

is 83 percent), and most of those persons are engaged in subsistence farming. A small minority of the population may raise cash crops, such as tea, coffee, cotton, fruit, and vegetables, but the major agricultural exports are produced on farms owned and managed by Europeans. The managerial and technical positions at oil and mining installations are held largely by foreigners; these modern installations are surrounded by backwardness. The life for the typical native is often tribally oriented and is sometimes nomadic.

These countries are characterized by a critical shortage of high-level manpower in all categories. Ethiopia, for example, has 2.2 primary and secondary teachers per 10,000 population and 0.10 physicians and dentists. (In the United States the figures are 135.1 teachers and 18.0 physicians and dentists.) Nonetheless, the largest single category of high-level manpower ordinarily is trained teachers. Top government posts are generally held by nationals, but technical positions in the public service, managerial, scientific, and engineering positions in commerce and industry, and many school posts as well are staffed by Europeans, Americans, and (in Africa) Asians.

The crust of custom is breaking, however. Public health measures have controlled some diseases, and infant mortality is falling. The resulting rise in population combines with a modest extension of primary school services and the building of roads to bring about a movement of people to the cities, where there is much overcrowding and unemployment.

Only about 20 to 30 percent of the 5-to-14 age group attend primary school, and the political pressure to expand these school services is often rather high. Apparently most children who enter primary school leave with no greater learning than bare literacy, a skill that lapses quite soon under the conditions of city slum or rural village life. Secondary school programs are generally of higher quality than those of the primary institutions. Only 2 to 5 percent of the relevant age group attend, but there is a chronic shortage of places. An infinitesimal number of nationals (relative to the age group) engage in higher education. Many schools at all levels are financed and administered by religious or voluntary agencies. In spite of this and in spite of the relatively small quantitative provision of educational services, expenditures on public education as a percentage of national income are of the same magnitude (4 to 6 percent) as in the richest countries of the world.

The category of partially developed countries—the other group of nations that are seriously interested in educational planning—consists of Guatemala, Burma, the Dominican Republic, China, Brazil, Pakistan, Iraq, and Turkey, among others. Per capita annual income in these countries sometimes reaches $300, but the average for the group is about $180. Compared with the underdeveloped countries, a smaller percentage of the population is engaged in agriculture, but it does not drop below 50 percent in any of the partially developed group. There is much greater evidence than in underdeveloped countries of the existence of a cash, or market, economy, and bank and financial systems are well developed. Urbanization is proceeding apace, and unemployment is often at a high level. These countries have some of the greatest rates of population increase in the world. Shortages of scientific, professional, and technical manpower are critical, as are shortages in subprofessional personnel such as engineers, agricultural technicians, nurses, secondary school teachers, and highly skilled craftsmen. The countries now manage to train a large supply of primary school teachers and nontechnical white-collar personnel, however.

Primary education has been expanded very rapidly, and it is not uncommon to find that over 50 percent of the 5-to-14 age group in these countries are enrolled in such programs. The problems at this level of education involve the quality of primary schooling and the extension of school services to backward rural areas. Because of the emphasis that governments have placed (a) on increasing the quantity of primary schooling and (b) on building university systems, the crucially important secondary level has been allowed to languish somewhat, and there is a severe shortage of places in secondary schools. The shortage is made to appear quantitatively high because of the rising number of applicants who appear on the scene from the primary institutions. Universities in the partially developed countries are expanding and are probably rising in quality at the same time.

What are some of the specific educational problems that countries in these two categories, underdeveloped and partially developed, face? The first is the difficulty of doing anything about improving education in the face of grinding poverty and a rapid increase in population. Yet there is political pressure to expand primary school services and there is national prestige to be garnered by developing good universities. Further, it is now taken as generally axiomatic that economic development requires an investment in education of the population. So these countries are going to continue to expand their educational services, and they are under extreme pressure to accomplish this expansion in an economically efficient manner.

This is not easy. Quantitative expansion of primary education requires the services of a larger number of teachers, but while a trained primary school teacher in the United States receives about 2 times the per capita national income, the primary school graduate who enters teaching in Ghana expects to get about 5 times the average income (in Nigeria it is 7 times). Expanding primary education is one of the most expensive things an undeveloped country can do, because education requires educated personnel and there is a high premium paid to educated people in these societies. This situation will gradually be changed as the supply of literate persons increases. "The primary school leaver's expectations derive not from the curriculum but from the status his immediate predecessors have enjoyed. In a developed country the wage of an unskilled laborer (which is all that primary education produces) is about one-third of the average income per occupied person; but a primary school leaver in Africa expects about twice the average income per occupied person. Obviously, if literacy became universal it would be impossible to pay every literate person twice the average income."[5] Not only is the expansion of primary education costly, but it thus carries the risk, if accomplished rapidly, of inducing much frustration among a growing number of primary school leavers who find that their status and income have been forced into a steady state of relative decline.

Moreover, it is questionable, even in the face of great political pressure, how much quantitative expansion of primary education there should be in the face of its qualitative deficiencies. Attrition rates over the course of the typical six-year program are extraordinarily high, and it is common practice for some children to repeat the first three grades several times before dropping out permanently. Little lasting effect on the pupils can be detected, and this makes the process of primary education wasteful, to say the least. But teachers typically have had no more than primary schooling themselves and many have not even completed primary school. Learning is often rote and may consist of memorizing a few Bible verses. Books and materials are scarce and deal with material far removed from the day-to-day experiences of the pupils. Part of the attrition rate can be explained by the low quality and irrelevance of instruction.

It would help if there could be more primary teachers who were trained to the level of secondary education. But expansion at the secondary level has not offered governments either great political support from the masses or the prestige of university expansion. Furthermore, many underdeveloped and partially developed countries are convinced that secondary education is academic in nature and is something conducted in a boarding school.[6] This boarding school concept increases the cost of capital facilities at the secondary level. In addition, the transfer of the English grammar school curriculum to underdeveloped countries may be fine for training future elementary school teachers, but it hardly provides for the education of other subprofessionals (craftsmen, draftsmen, agricultural technicians, medical technicians). It is these subprofessionals who are urgently needed for the economic development of the countries. Some vocational secondary schools exist, but because of the general shortage of secondary school places and the high status that goes with graduation from any type of secondary school, applicants turned away from high-grade academic secondary schools flock into these slightly lower-status vocational institutions. These students have no real intention of ever becoming craftsmen or tech-

---

[5] W. Arthur Lewis, "Education and Economic Development," *International Social Science Journal,* XIV, No. 4 (1962), p. 688.
    [6] *Ibid.,* p. 691.

nicians; their secondary graduation qualifies them for administrative or clerical posts, which is what they wanted in the first place.

At the university level, underdeveloped and partially developed countries face further serious choices. Shall national universities be expanded or shall young people be encouraged to obtain their higher education in the universities of the advanced countries? Often the latter alternative provides better education at lower cost all around. But local universities serve a number of functions besides instruction: provision for research about local problems, participation of the faculty in the intellectual, cultural, and business life of the community, and so on. There is some feeling that the programs tend to over-emphasize the humanities, arts, and law and neglect the disciplines of science, engineering, agriculture, and medicine. There is also some tendency for the number of institutions and separate facilities to be proliferated so that costs become quite high.[7]

These are some of the problems that the poorer countries face in trying to expand their educational services in an efficient manner. To help in the process of expanding education it is now common practice for these countries to develop an "educational plan," which is closely geared to the plans for the economic development of the nation. We now turn to a brief consideration of some of the techniques of drawing up educational plans.

THE TECHNIQUE OF EDUCATIONAL PLANNING

The development of a national education plan logically begins with the accumulation of certain types of background information. This information can be described as a "manpower inventory."[8] Data apply to the current time period. The following types of statistical estimates are included in a manpower inventory: labor force participation rates by five-year age groups and sex; estimates of unemployment; occupation distribution of employed workers by branch of industry and sex; educational qualifications of employed workers by occupation; and distribution of labor force by level of education, age, and sex. The uses of these kinds of information will become clear as we see what the other steps in educational planning are.

The next task in educational planning is to make a forecast of the size of the total labor force at the "target date," ordinarily a time fifteen years in the future. First this calls for a forecast of population, not a difficult task if reliable data on the numbers and ages of people already born are available, because

---

[7]Harbison and Myers, op. cit., p. 85.

[8]This statement follows the widely accepted procedure laid out in Herbert S. Parnes, *Forecasting Educational Needs for Economic and Social Development* (Paris: Organization for Economic Cooperation and Development, 1962).

the economically active population in most countries is over fourteen years of age. More difficult problems center on changes in the labor force participation rate (basic data are included in the manpower inventory for this estimate) —changes related to opportunities for part-time work, retirement age, and average length of school life.

The next step is to estimate total employment by branch of industry. This is best done by preparing an estimate of gross national product (itself a technical procedure which makes use of forecast of civilian labor force, noted just above, and productivity change) and then allocating this future GNP to branches of industry (agriculture, mining, manufacturing, business services, public services, and so on). In allocating the GNP it is generally helpful to consider the present production structure in countries that are slightly more advanced economically than one's own. Finally, these output measures are converted into employment estimates by branch of industry, taking account of expected changes in hours worked per year and man-hour productivity.

One is then ready to prepare estimates of the occupational composition of the future labor force by branch of industry. That is, one seeks to discover how many different types of skills are going to be needed in the various productive sectors of the economy: how many medical doctors, teachers, engineers, carpenters, writers, machinists, agricultural technicians, and so on, there are to be. For certain high-level occupations, the computation requires nothing but converting the stated policies of the government into numbers. For instance, if it is the policy to have 5 medical doctors per 10,000 population by 1985, the forecast of this occupational category is a matter of simple arithmetic (assuming that population forecasts themselves are available). For factory work, it is practical to consider how occupational structure is changing in the more progressive local plants and in the more efficient foreign plants. Educational planning has progressed to the point where one has a realistic forecast of how many people are to be employed in various occupations in the target year.

The next step is to estimate the educational requirements (or educational prerequisites) for all the various occupations that will exist in the economy at the target date. This sounds formidable, but two things should be noted: (1) existing levels of educational preparation of persons in various occupations have already been examined in the manpower inventory and (2) for long-range forecasts (for example, fifteen years ahead) it is sufficient to know the numbers of people with various levels of education that will be required — to state the requirements in terms of so many primary school graduates, secondary graduates, and university graduates. Then, as one moves toward the target date, the requirements are stated with greater specificity, first in terms of broad types of secondary programs (general vs. technical) and later in terms of specific occupational training programs. But the closer one is to the target date, the easier it becomes to specify educational prerequisities.

Next, the object is to estimate the supply of persons in various occupational groups in the target year, taking account of present numbers employed (from the manpower inventory), anticipated outflows from the educational system under the scheme of existing educational policies, and losses due to death, retirement, and withdrawal from the labor force. Presumably there will be some discrepancies between anticipated demand for personnel in the target year, as computed above, and the estimate of anticipated supply. For example, it may be found that an expansion of secondary schooling is called for. This may or may not require, in turn, an expansion of primary education, but it is almost certain to require a prior increase in either university training or normal school training in order to provide a larger number of secondary school teachers. Using arithmetic models, the objective is to discover those revisions in educational policy that will close the gaps between the estimated demand for educated persons and the estimated supply. Basically, one comes out with a set of figures showing how many children are to be encouraged to enter particular types of educational programs at particular points of time. And of course one must allow for attrition both during the period of schooling and between school and work. Rates of attrition will probably differ by sex and may differ in urban and rural schools.

What has been described here in broad terms is a simple model of educational planning. More sophisticated models would take account of the fact that the "periods of production" for developing various intellectual skills may show differences by type of student or by geographic area; indeed, they may be subject to change by improvements in pedagogical techniques.

Some people may feel it is detestable that the educational opportunities made available to children are functions of the future manpower requirements of a country, but it is no accident that the first real application of educational planning has occurred in Africa, Asia, the Middle East, and South America. The countries are desperately poor, and extension of education is extraordinarily expensive to accomplish. It is morally wrong that educational policies should be developed haphazardly and that educational practices should be wasteful. Furthermore, what is developed through educational planning is a kind of minimum efficient program. If a country wishes to expand its educational programs further to reap cultural advantages for its people, that remains its choice.

Suggested Readings

BURTLE, J. "Input-Output Analysis as an Aid to Manpower Policy." *International Labor Review*, May 1952.

CORREA, H., and TINBERGEN, J. "Quantitative Adaptation of Education to Accelerated Growth," *Kyklos*, No. 4, 1962.

HARBISON, FREDERICK, and MYERS, CHARLES A. *Education, Manpower and Economic Growth*. New York: McGraw-Hill, 1964.

National Manpower Council. *Public Policies and Manpower Resources*. New York: Columbia Univ. Press, 1964.

Organization for Economic Cooperation and Development. *Policy Conference on Economic Growth and Investment in Education*. Washington: Government Printing Office, 1962.

PARNES, HERBERT S. *Forecasting Educational Needs for Economic and Social Development*. Paris: Organization for Economic Cooperation and Development, 1962.

Chapter Ten: EFFICIENCY IN AMERICAN EDUCATION

THE COMPLEXITY OF THE CASE

We have just seen that underdeveloped countries seek to improve the efficiency of their educational enterprises by adjusting the size and structure of the educational system in accordance with the manpower requirements of their economies. Educational planning in these nations may be warped by political pressures; it is certainly hampered by the difficulties of estimating the future demands for—and supplies of—educated manpower; but the basic objectives and techniques of planning are straightforward enough. In the United States matters are more complicated, in part because the economy is so dynamic and in part because educational administration at all levels—elementary, secondary, and higher—is extremely decentralized. Nonetheless, the manifold importance of the educational services, as well as the vast quantities of economic resources they consume, argues for consideration of efficiency criteria in even so rich a country as America. In the following discussion, efficiency problems will be treated under two headings: process and distribution.

EFFICIENT EDUCATIONAL PROCESSES

Economic criteria for efficient production were stated in general terms in Chapter 3, and here we will analyze the allocation of resources among competing uses within a local school district. Applying the economic logic to decisions about educational processes, we seek the situation (in the abstract) where the last dollar allocated to each of the various types of production resources (teachers of various qualifications, specialists, administrators, books, chalk, projectors, laboratories and laboratory equipment, libraries, librarians, and all the rest) yields an equal return in meeting the objectives of the local district. This kind of statement, however, is theoretical, so let us consider a slightly more realistic situation.

Suppose a school district has established as one of its objectives that, subject to budgetary constraints, only the smallest possible number of third-graders will fail to achieve a defined standard in reading proficiency. Assume that the state has directed that all districts give third-grade pupils a standard test in reading comprehension, and suppose that our particular district has chosen to minimize the number of pupils who receive scores below the lower quartile of the statewide distribution of scores. The minimum acceptable score (call it MAS) is defined, then, as Q_1 by state standards. Next let us assume that for several years past the district has had exactly 100 pupils who have scored below the MAS.

It has been determined that the employment of a specialist teacher in reading will reduce the number of low-scoring pupils by 30 and that the employment of one additional preprimary teacher will reduce the number by 20. Say that the cost of employing the reading specialist (salary, fringes, special materials) is $9000 and the cost of engaging the preprimary teacher is $7000. The average cost of raising a pupil above the MAS by employing a reading specialist is $300; by employing the preprimary teacher, $350. Ordinary logic would suggest that the district should employ the reading specialist at this point.

Suppose that (a) the district is still not satisfied with its attempt to bring pupils up to the MAS, (b) the only known procedures for accomplishing this objective are the employment of reading specialists or preprimary teachers, and (c) the cost of hiring additional numbers of these persons remains constant. The number of children below the MAS has been cut to 70 (as a result of hiring the one additional specialist teacher). At this point one more specialist teacher would reduce the number of pupils that are below the MAS by 22, and one more preprimary teacher would cut it by 18. The per-pupil cost of raising scores above the MAS in reading proficiency by employing a specialist teacher is $409, and by employing a preprimary teacher, $389. At this stage the district should hire the preprimary teacher.

This little arithmetic example is illustrative of an important line of reasoning. A school district provides a set of services using a large assortment of human and physical resources. As soon as the district seeks to expand its services so that it can meet old objectives more fully or strive toward certain new objectives, the district is well advised to weigh the marginal contribution of alternative factor inputs relative to the costs of those factors at each convenient stage of expansion of output. In the first stage of our example, it would have been poor economy for the district to hire the cheaper teacher; in the second stage, it would have been poor economy to hire the teacher who brought the larger absolute number of children above the MAS. Stage by stage, the district can move as close to the attainment of its objective as it considers desirable (up to the point, for example, where all 100 children score above the MAS). By weighing marginal contributions relative to marginal costs of alternative factor inputs, the district achieves the desired level of attainment at minimum cost, thus having more money left over to do other desirable things. Economically speaking, there is likely to be no one best way to accomplish an objective (specialist teachers are not necessarily the single answer to correcting reading difficulties of pupils); rather, one must take account of what one is already accomplishing, what educational resources are available to expand services, and what the incremental contribution of each type of newly added resource is, relative to its cost.

In reaching this conclusion we are making a number of assumptions, and it is worth noting what they are. First, it is assumed that the objectives of school districts can be rather precisely stated. Second, it is assumed that the units in which the objectives are achieved can be defined. Third, it is assumed that the variables which influence the achievement of the objective can be identified and, further, that the units of these variables can be defined and priced. Fourth, and most difficult, it is assumed that the relation between the input variables and the number of units of achievement of the objectives can be specified at each level of output.[1]

But matters in education are never even this simple. Ordinarily there are multiple objectives that are achieved more or less simultaneously (children are taught both reading and arithmetic in the same short stretch of hours in a school day, for example), and ordinarily several input variables are jointly employed. In the abstract these complications can be taken care of by programing techniques, as illustrated in the appendix to this chapter.

In more general terms, one obtains efficient allocations of resources in education by either of two procedures: One sets certain standards of output —call these standards of pupil achievement—and then by a process of trial and error determines which combinations of resources appear to meet these

---

[1]Kenneth M. Deitch, "Some Observations on the Allocation of Resources in Higher Education," *Review of Economics and Statistics*, Supplement, August 1960, p. 196.

standards at lowest cost; or one sets certain standards of expenditure and, once again by a process of trial or error, determines which combinations of resources yield the largest gains in certain defined types of output. The thing to avoid is a confusion of the two procedures. One might hear the following sort of statement from a school official: "We want to have a well-run school system. What we want to do is have the greatest impact on the largest number of children at minimum cost." This "greatest good for the greatest number" approach only serves to confound efforts to obtain a rational distribution of scarce resources.

Common sense will dictate that certain errors of planning should be avoided. One error is the neglect of "spill-over effects." Mastery of skills in one discipline may increase the student's capacity to perform in other fields. Then extra-large expenditures on instruction in the basic discipline may be economically justified. A second type of error is ignoring valuable inputs. This is particularly easy to do in education where some inputs, such as the time of pupils, are not priced in the market.

A third source of error can be the improper allocation of joint costs. The general rule is to regard incremental (or marginal) costs as the guiding figures. Suppose there is a proposal to build a laboratory in a high school that could be used as a chemistry lab or a biology lab, or for both purposes. Let the basic cost of the laboratory be $100,000. Assume it costs an additional $60,000 to fit out the facility as a chemistry lab and $40,000 to provide the biology equipment. Under what conditions should the lab be built, and should it be a single or a joint facility? It should be constructed if its value in the instruction of chemistry exceeds $160,000, if its value for biology students exceeds $140,000, or if its value to both together exceeds $200,000. If its value in both fields combined exceeds $200,000, it should be constructed for joint use as long as its value for chemistry exceeds $60,000 (the difference between the cost of joint tenancy, $200,000, and the cost of the lab fitted just for biology, $140,000) and its value for biology exceeds $40,000 ($200,000 − $160,000).[2]

Not all discussion about economic efficiency in education is so abstract. In Chapter 7 we observed that a person may question in general terms whether education should have remained so highly labor-intensive for so long —questioned, that is, whether productivity in the classroom could not be raised by greater use of equipment and materials. The economist is disposed to raise such questions, but only educational research can answer them. In the next chapter we shall have something to say about whether specialization in the performance of educational tasks should be extended; this is also a question of general, though not technical, interest to the economist.

[2]Charles J. Hitch and Roland N. McKean, *The Economics of Defense in the Nuclear Age* (Cambridge, Mass.: Harvard Univ. Press, 1961), pp. 173–74.

EFFICIENT GEOGRAPHIC DISTRIBUTION
OF EDUCATIONAL RESOURCES

So far we have been looking at the question of the allocation of resources within an individual school district. Another efficiency problem is the distribution of educational resources among school districts. Apparently the distribution of educational resources in the United States is quite uneven. Among the states, expenditures for public elementary and secondary schools per pupil in average daily attendance varied from $790 in New York to $273 in Mississippi (1964–65). Average teachers' salaries in 1964–65 varied from $7550 in California to $3975 in Mississippi. Differences in class size were also notable, and so were variations in capital outlay.

On the face of it, differences in expenditures within states are also quite shocking. Let us consider the case of Massachusetts, since the commonwealth can properly be regarded as the cradle of free public education in the United States. In 1949–50 the range in expenditure per "weighted classroom" ran from $2500 to $8300.[3] Expenditures at the upper level were 3.3 times those at the lower. In 1959–60 the range was $5075 to $12,075. The upper limit was still 2.4 times the lower. In California, a state with a much newer (or more recently developed) educational system—and also our largest —the picture is similar. In 1949–50 the expenditure range was from $1100 to $12,100; in 1959–60 it remained substantial: $3670 to $15,910.

But one cannot be surprised about such figures. In Chapter 7 we noted that the dynamic element in educational expenditure is change in teachers' salaries. One would expect some districts to be more aggressive in competing for teachers' services than others. Further, some districts have greater financial resources than others. By and large, local school expenditures are related significantly to the wealth or financial ability of the districts.

Indeed, the teacher looking for his first post will note that some districts offer relatively low salaries, and these are the same districts in which he stands a good chance of being assigned an overcrowded class, of teaching in an old, poorly maintained school building, and of having to make do with a meager supply of auxiliary services, such as library facilities. The high-salaried districts in his state are the ones in which class size is typically small, buildings are bright and clean, and auxiliary services relatively abundant. Naturally enough, the economically favored districts have a much wider circle of applicants from

---

[3]The notion of "weighted classroom" as the unit of expenditure measure is simply a device to allow comparisons to be made among districts which may serve only elementary pupils and districts which serve only secondary pupils, because expenditures are generally higher (per pupil) at the secondary level than at the elementary. See Clayton Hutchins and Albert R. Munse, *Expenditures for Education at the Midcentury* (Washington: Government Printing Office, 1953).

which to choose than do the disadvantaged ones. The rich district can choose among candidates who have had the benefit of being trained in the most prestigious colleges and universities of the land and who have had the experience one gains by extensive travel. The poor district will have rather few candidates and most of these will be persons who have grown up in the immediate area and had all their schooling not far from their birthplace. These persons must necessarily have some attachment to their immediate geographic area which motivates them to offer their services in the disadvantaged district.

There is another reason why the difference in caliber of staff between rich and poor schools may have widened in the postwar years. The quality of secondary education has risen, most notably in the college-preparatory curriculum. The improvement has been stimulated by efforts of the federal government, acting through the National Science Foundation, to upgrade instruction in mathematics, science, and modern languages. Not all secondary schools have shown the same rate of improvement, since some are more closely linked into a national network of communication than others are. "The academic offerings of our high schools appear to have been strengthened. However, schools in rural areas and serving populations of lower socioeconomic status have not benefited as much as the more favored schools, with a result of widening the gap that may already have existed between them."[4] The affluent schools draw candidates who have been through superior secondary schools and who have gone on to further study in our great universities. The depressed school system has not shared very much in the improvement in secondary education, but its own products are its future teachers. These secondary school graduates, moreover, face an increasing handicap in gaining admission to a first-rate institution of higher education because their high school preparation has lagged behind the times.

The favoring of the richer, more educationally progressive schools can be defended as a matter of policy. "The world needs people with superior education. Everyone has an interest . . . in the existence and the efficient use of people with the highest of training. Excellence in diplomacy, statesmanship, art, science, medicine, architecture, entertainment, religion, judicial decision, national defense, or economics requires great skill. It calls for extensive training. Not many school districts can afford top-quality elementary or secondary schooling . . . but some communities are able and willing to provide much more than others . . . Inequality makes possible a kind of accomplishment for the whole society which would not be attainable under conditions of equality."[5]

---

[4]R. F. Campbell and R. A. Bunnell, "Differential Impact of National Programs on Secondary Schools," *School Review*, Winter 1963, p. 476.

[5]C. Lowell Harriss, "Comments," in National Bureau of Economic Research, *Public Finances: Needs, Sources, and Utilization* (Princeton, N.J.: Princeton Univ. Press, 1961), p. 130.

Apparently this is the rationale under which we have been operating in American education up to this time.

Yet, even on a simple matter of economic policy, it may now be appropriate to right the balance and to seek improvement, especially in the programs of disadvantaged schools. Otherwise we may not be able to move forward toward the goal of full employment. We will be hampered by bottlenecks in the supply of skilled production workers (who do not, generally speaking, go to school in the affluent suburbs) and by the difficulty of finding jobs in a technological age for people who are barely literate, verbally and numerically.[6]

APPENDIX TO CHAPTER 10

Programing of the Allocation of Educational Resources

Assume there are two subjects in which a group of academically homogeneous pupils are being instructed; call them Subject 1 and Subject 2. (These might be numerical calculation and arithmetic reasoning.) Assume that it is possible to define units of proficiency in each subject, and to establish minimum acceptable standards of proficiency for this particular group of children. There are two methods of instruction employed; call them A and B. (One might be desk and board work from text problems and the other might be work with physical models in a "math lab.") The method of instruction and units of proficiency are related as shown in the following table.

TABLE XIII

HYPOTHETICAL RELATION OF METHOD OF INSTRUCTION TO UNITS OF PROFICIENCY

Subject	Amount of Proficiency Provided by One Unit of		Minimum Standard of Proficiency
	Method A	Method B	
1	2	1	14
2	1	2	16

---

[6] In fact, it has been suggested that the United States should use the educational planning techniques that underdeveloped countries employ. See R. S. Eckaus, "Economic Criteria for Education and Training," *Review of Economics and Statistics*, May 1964, pp. 181–90. Such an emphasis on regulating the distribution of educational resources in accordance with manpower requirements would almost certainly create a distribution different from the one we now have. A certain amount of data for the implementation of such an approach has been prepared: U.S. Department of Labor, *Estimates of Worker Trait Requirements for 4,000 Jobs* (Washington: Government Printing Office, 1960).

In this table it should be noted that "minimum standards of proficiency" does not necessarily refer to low standards; it is simply a way of stating standards of performance "at least as high as . . . ," and these can be set
quite high. The problem is to determine the most efficient combination of
instructional methods A and B to achieve these minimum standards of performance. The most efficient combination might be determined in terms of
the dollar cost of providing units of instructional methods A and B for students. Alternatively, it might be that combination of the two instructional
methods that would allow students to achieve the minimum levels of achievement at least cost to themselves in terms of their own time. (After all, the
student's own time is the scarcest of all educational resources in an advanced
economy.) If this combination can be stated for the indicated levels of
achievement in Subjects 1 and 2, it could probably be stated for other levels of
the same subject and for various levels of other subjects as well, so that the
students generally are led to make the most effective use of the hours they
devote to learning.

The procedure for solution is indicated graphically in Fig. 7. Line 1 represents all those combinations of instructional methods A and B that meet
the minimum requirement in Subject 1. For example, the requirement can be
met by employing 7 units of method A and zero units of method B, by 6 units
of method A and 2 units of method B, and so on up to 14 units of method B
and zero units of method A. Similarly, line 2 represents all combinations of
methods A and B that yield the minimum requirement in Subject 2. The
shaded area of the chart—the area above and to the right of the two lines
just described—represents all combinations of these two methods of instruction that meet or exceed minimum requirements of learning.

Suppose that a unit of method A and a unit of method B each require
one hour of a student's time. What is the minimum amount of time necessary

FIG. 7

GRAPHIC SOLUTION OF SCHOOL RESOURCE ALLOCATION PROBLEM

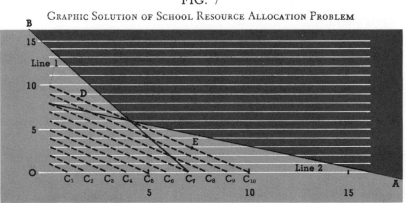

to achieve the proficiency requirement, and what combination of the two methods of instruction requires the minimum expenditure of time? Obviously, we seek a point somewhere on the heavy line of Fig. 7. No point closer to the origin satisfies the proficiency requirement, and any point above or to the right of this line exceeds them. Let us draw a series of parallel lines, $C_1, C_2, C_3, \ldots, C_{10}$, each showing the various combinations of instructional methods A and B that can be had by using the total number of hours indicated in the subscript of the symbol that identifies each line. For example, with a total of 3 hours (C_3), it is possible to have 3 hours of method A and zero hours of method B, 2 hours of method A and 1 hour of method B, 1 hour of method A and 2 hours of method B, and so on. As the lines are placed progressively to the right, a larger total of instructional hours is consumed. We want to identify the C line that touches the heavy line of minimum instructional requirements and is closest to the origin. Any line of instructional hours that touches the heavy broken line provides enough instructional time for the learning requirements to be met; of those that touch it, the one closest to the origin represents the *smallest number of hours in which the require-ments can be met*. In Fig. 7 the C line we require is C_{10}. The combination of instructional hours indicated is 4 hours of method A and 6 hours of method B. The problem indicated in Table I is solved. Note also that it is possible to use (or misuse) ten hours of instructional time in the wrong combination of methods. Points D and E on the C_{10} line yield less than the minimum standard of output of instruction in one subject or another, as you can readily check.[7]

Suggested Readings

BENSON, CHARLES S. *State-Local Fiscal Cooperation in Education in California.* Sacramento, Calif.: Senate Fact-Finding Committee on Revenue and Taxation, 1965.

BURKHEAD, JESSE. *Government Budgeting.* New York: Wiley, 1956.

DEITCH, KENNETH M. "Some Observations on the Allocating of Resources in Higher Education," *Review of Economics and Statistics,* Supplement, August 1960.

KERSHAW, JOSEPH A., and McKEAN, ROLAND N. *Systems Analysis and Education.* Santa Monica, Calif.: Rand Corp., 1959.

MINER, JERRY. *Social and Economic Factors in Spending for Public Education.* Syracuse, N.Y.: Syracuse Univ. Press, 1964.

WASSERMAN, WILLIAM. *Education Price and Quantity Indexes.* Syracuse, N.Y.: Syracuse Univ. Press, 1964.

---

[7] This is a simple example of "linear programing." As long as certain mathematical relations hold among variables, it is possible to apply a technique of solution to the problem of minimizing (or maximizing) some "objective function" when the number of choice variables (or inputs) is large and when the number of constraints —for example, minimum requirements— is also large. The technique uses algebra, not graphs, of course. See Robert Dorfman, Paul A. Samuelson, and Robert M. Solow, *Linear Programing and Economic Analysis* (New York: McGraw-Hill, 1958); and William Wasserman, *Education Price and Quantity Indexes* (Syracuse, N.Y.: Syracuse Univ. Press, 1963), pp. 135–46.

Chapter Eleven: ECONOMIC PROBLEMS OF PUBLIC EDUCATION

THE RESPONSIBILITY OF TEACHERS IN POLICYMAKING

It is hoped that no one has read this book without gaining the feeling, if he did not have it already, that the quality of our national life is strongly related to the quality and distribution of the educational services. In addition, it is reasonable to conclude that the successful implementation of national economic policy is becoming *increasingly* dependent upon the activities of educational agencies. Teachers and principals have kinds of information that are not normally available to the central administration of local school districts or to state or federal school administrators. In the view of the author, educational policy has become too important to be left in the hands of full-time administrators (and the lay boards to which they are accountable). But if teachers and principals continue to expand their roles as critics—and occasionally as instigators—of policy, it is crucial that they be informed, not just about what the conditions are within their school and school district, but also about the changing role of school services on the national scene. And, hopefully, informed debates among teachers about policy issues will rise in number, because discussion is a primary means of sharpening understanding in the field of policy.

This chapter deals briefly with some of the major policy issues in education today, emphasizing of course the economic aspects of these problems. Bias of the author will be evident, but "final answers" are not intended here; rather, the problems will be stated and some of their ramifications explored.

CENTRALIZATION VS. LOCAL AUTONOMY

We start with a problem that might be discussed just as well by a political scientist as by an economist, but the fact is that the issue of centralization vs. local control is an extraordinarily convenient one under which to raise a number of economic "subproblems." And anyway, economists have long been interested in matters dealing with "industrial structure"; here we are simply concerned with structure in the public sector.

Traditionally, localism in education has been defended mainly on two grounds: (a) decentralization in policymaking allows school authorities to design their programs specifically to meet local needs (it is assumed that needs vary in some important ways from one school district to another), and (b) freedom of local authorities from detailed central direction fosters experimentation (it is further assumed that the kind of experimentation which school districts carry out is favorable for the improvement of the educational services).[1] Let us examine each of these claims briefly.

As to the claim that local government can meet local needs, one can legitimately ask whose needs are being met effectively. In recent years it has become clear that some school administrations in our large cities have provided a more favorable distribution of educational resources to schools which serve the middle and upper classes than to schools that serve children from slum neighborhoods. One can make a case that it is really these latter schools that should receive the more generous allowance (we shall shortly consider some of these arguments). It is, generally, the state and federal governments, not the local government, that have taken the initiative to alter the distribution of resources in favor of schools in disadvantaged neighborhoods through, for example, the compensatory education acts of various states and the federal government's Elementary and Secondary Education Act of 1965.

---

[1]Deliberately, we leave out another argument — that local government offers participation in political activities to many citizens who would otherwise lack an opportunity to share in such activities, and that local government is therefore a training ground for democracy. We do not deal with this argument because it applies to local government generally, not just to education, and because it raises difficult questions in the field of political science about what types of citizen participation are most favorable for developing a sense of — and a craft for — responsible government.

As to the claim that local control fosters experimentation, let us recognize first of all that local districts have never been successful in raising any large amount of money for educational research. Experimentation conducted in the absence of an adequately financed design of research is unlikely to yield clear-cut findings, findings of a type that can be reported and defended under rigorous examination; thus the building of a science of education has proceeded quite haltingly. Yet it is not to be expected that a local district would find it prudent to invest large sums in research. Research is risky because only a fraction of projects yield useful new knowledge. Research bears fruit only in the long run. The findings theoretically benefit pupils in many districts, not just those in the locality which provided the money to support the investigation.[2]

On the other hand, research expenditures for education by the federal government have expanded from practically nothing to something in excess of $150 million per annum in the ten-year period 1955–1965. Leadership in educational experimentation has gravitated to the federal government; in part this is because of its superior financial resources. This fact raises another problem, however. How are teachers to be made aware of advances in knowledge about instruction? Local districts, notwithstanding the modest recognition given in salary schedules to advanced training, have not really succeeded in offering promotions — in salary or responsibility — to those particular teachers who manage to keep up with the new developments in their field of teaching. Clear rewards are not laid before the teacher who participates fully in the scientific advance of education. Furthermore, local districts have done relatively little to provide full- or half-year paid leaves to teachers in order that they may undertake retraining in a serious, not casual or summer school, manner.[3]

One may hold some reservations about the main arguments for local control. However, our structure of education has probably one major accomplishment to its credit — it has proved effective in raising the huge sums of money required for a vast extension of educational services. Though our cultural tradition is not, relatively speaking, particularly old or rich, we have an educational system under which the student is offered more years of schooling, free of fees, than he is offered in any other country in the world. (In Chapter 8 we noted that this extension has apparently accounted for a significant

---

[2]That is, there are strong external benefits provided when a single local authority expends money on a well-designed research program, although the district has no means of recouping its investment from the other districts that will benefit equally from its investigations. In private industry this problem is ameliorated to some degree by patent and copyright protection; obviously these semimonopolistic practices have no place in the public sector.

[3]Teachers will not necessarily remain in the employment of the district which met the cost of their sabbaticals long enough for that district to recoup its "investment." Therefore, as in financing educational research, many of the benefits of retraining are external.

share of our economic growth, but the extension had to be paid for in advance of reaping the economic returns.) In our earlier history local school authorities were allowed a loose rein in establishing secondary schools, and though many of these early efforts in extending the years of schooling were of doubtful value, the idea of universal secondary education caught hold and a kind of miracle of educational provision (as judged by European authorities) was accomplished. These facts show that local autonomy is an effective means for voicing the general demands for public services.

Allowing this point, let us recognize that the task of extending educational provision in the United States has been largely accomplished. Does localism still make sense in our society? On the financial side, local control implies that individual authorities have a source of revenue at their command—a tax instrument which is theirs to administer. It has not been possible to discover a levy other than the property tax which can be used by small local authorities. This instrument, however, is regressive and has other unfortunate features, as we noted in Chapter 6. Worse still, most of our states have quite large numbers of school districts, and this implies that the differences in financial resources — that is, taxable capacity — among districts will be large. It has not been possible to devise a system of grants-in-aid that can fully compensate for large differences in local fiscal capacity. To provide a given expenditure per pupil, tax rates are ordinarily higher in poor districts than in rich. Correspondingly, expenditures per pupil are ordinarily higher in rich districts than in poor, even though it is probable that a dollar goes farther in the richer districts.[4] All of this is apparently inequitable, but the situation has existed for a long time. Certain emphases in national economic policy, however, appear to call for a change in the geographic distribution of educational resources, as we will now consider.

The federal government is taking a number of steps to raise the nation's economic productivity. (We noted some of these steps in Chapter 5.) Indeed, the government is more or less forced into this position because other nations are showing substantial productivity advances; our position as a world power requires that we do equally well. At the same time the federal government has committed itself to the goal of full employment. To achieve a rapid advance in productivity and full employment is not easy. It is important that there be an adequate supply of highly skilled foremen and craftsmen, in order that expansion of progressive firms not be inhibited by critical labor shortages. But the problem runs deeper than this. Advances in productivity are most likely

---

[4]Suppose a pleasant suburban school district and one in an old industrial town had identical salary schedules. Which district would be likely to attract the better-qualified teachers? Probably the surburban district. Should the old industrial town decide it wanted as good teachers as the suburb had, it would probably have to offer higher salaries than did its more fortunate neighbor.

to occur in agriculture, mining, and manufacturing. These are the very industries that have offered employment of a routine, repetitive character to great numbers of people with minimum levels of education. One cannot expect demand for foodstuffs and manufactured goods to expand at such a rate that there will not be a relative contraction of employment (as distinct from output) in these major industries. Persons with minimum levels of education henceforth must look in large numbers to the service industries for employment. But educational prerequisites for employment in the lower ranks of service trades (appliance repairmen, service station attendants, cooks, and waiters) are somewhat higher than in the lower ranks of agriculture, mining, and manufacturing. Thus the educational threshold for steady employment is rising.

When we consider the future supply of skilled workers and craftsmen and the numbers of young people who will seek lower-grade jobs in the service industries, we are considering primarily persons who are unlikely to attend a four-year institution of higher education. In the years of their elementary and secondary schooling many of these young people will be living in school districts of less than average wealth. It is just such districts that have difficulty obtaining their fair share of educational resources under our decentralized system of public education, but somehow these districts must provide higher-quality education than they have in the past; otherwise the non-college-bound youth of the land will not be encouraged to cross over the rising educational threshold for stable employment.[5] Therefore the twin national goals of rising productivity and full employment will be hard to meet. To make matters even more difficult, it is well known that some children are better prepared, relatively speaking, to enter school than others are. The districts that are handicapped in their supply of educational resources and that nonetheless need to do better by their pupils than they did in the past are likely to be ones with a high proportion of pupils from homes where reading and other intellectual skills are not stressed. The hard-pressed district, then, even were it well endowed with school resources, would have to try harder to raise the educational standards of its pupils than the district with average socioeconomic status. National economic policy may suggest, then, a different geographic distribution of educational resources from the one our rather laissez-faire system of decentralized control has provided, with greater resources being made available to those districts that serve large numbers of the less academically oriented youth (or to those that have a large proportion of such youths in their total enrollment).

---

[5]There is no indication that the training needs of these youths will be met in significant degree by their future employers. In general, it is the larger firms that have well-established formal training programs. The shift of employment toward service industries is a shift toward an industrial sector in which the average size of firms is rather small. In itself, this augurs poorly for the extension of on-the-job training.

ECONOMIC PROBLEMS IN PERSONNEL PRACTICES

Francis Keppel, Assistant Secretary of Health, Education, and Welfare, has recently written, "We must face the fact that the personnel structure of the schools is ill designed to attract or to hold anything like an adequate proportion of the nation's most skilled and promising young men and women. This is true above all when other professions will be in need of the very same group. For salaries are not only too low—they also do not offer enough range. They tend to assume that all teachers are the same, and all teaching jobs alike. Common sense, of course, denies the former; alas, the present situation does not deny the latter. A widening of the range would seem to call for a change in the structure."[6]

Shortages of personnel appear to be particularly acute in the fields of mathematics, science, and vocational-technical education.[7] These are of course the fields in which young potential teachers are likely to receive attractive offers from private industry. By and large, school districts refuse to meet the industrial competition; they refuse, that is, to pay more money to a teacher of mathematics or science than to a teacher of, say, social studies (assuming both have the same number of years of experience and of training). But the shortage exists in those very fields where it is crucial that the young person receive good basic instruction as a foundation for his future work skills.

One does not have to look far to see other evidences of malfunctioning of personnel policy in education. Moonlighting, euphemistically called "dual jobholding" by the U.S. Department of Labor, exists at a higher rate among male schoolteachers than among any other occupational group, not even excluding such protective workers as night watchmen.[8] Too many teachers, it would appear, find it necessary (or satisfying) to channel a share of their work energy and ambition into lines of endeavor only remotely connected with the main position for which they have been trained. This is economically wasteful.

The responsibilities of a professional position in education have not been clearly defined. In a school district it is often difficult to determine where the responsibility of the classroom teachers ends and the responsibilities of the directors, coordinators, supervisors, consultants, principals, and various categories of superintendent begin. Such lack of classification can be distracting to those who are honestly seeking to carry on the work of the system; it can also

---

[6]Francis Keppel, *Personnel Policies for Public Education* (Horace Mann Lecture, 1961; Pittsburgh: Univ. of Pittsburgh, 1961).

[7]The problem is not that we have empty mathematics and science classrooms, but that the people teaching these subject often have had very little work in the field they are trying to teach. See Joseph A. Kershaw and Roland N. McKean, *Teacher Shortages and Salary Schedules* (New York: McGraw-Hill, 1962).

[8]We are not referring here to teachers who take summer or Christmas jobs, but to those who have two or more jobs during the regular school year.

be a subterfuge for the avoidance of responsibility. The most important effect of this lack of definition is that schools have never arrived at an effective division of labor, under which each person spends most of his working day at those tasks — but only those tasks — that call upon his highest skills (natural and acquired).

Team teaching, merit pay, and various specialty plans are attempts to meet some of the problems of personnel in education. Nothing yet devised appears adequate to the task.

METROPOLITANISM AND SCHOOL GOVERNMENT

We are becoming ever more an urban nation. Recognizing this, let us point out that a metropolis is more than a collection of suburbs. The cultural and financial life of a metropolitan region is fostered in the "central city." These central cities, moreover, are home for vast multitudes of people, most of whom have nowhere else to go. (There is, as well, a growing minority of relatively affluent adults who choose to live in the city, which reflects a taste for urban living that Europeans have enjoyed for many decades.)

It is commonplace to say that the central cities are in trouble, but it is not easy to find the roots of their difficulty. Costs of government admittedly are high. Let us look first at the school services. Salary costs per teacher are likely to be slightly higher in the central city than in the suburbs, even though schedule maximums are relatively low. This situation is accounted for mainly by two conditions: (a) central cities have many older teachers, that is, persons who are at maximum scheduled salary, and (b) beginning salaries in the central cities typically are high, because cities need to recruit a large number of new teachers each year simply to satisfy the demands of their large school systems. Next, central cities face very high costs for the acquisition of sites on which to build new schools or construct extensions of old schools. A third cost-increasing factor is that central cities have a relatively large proportion of their students enrolled in vocational and technical programs. These programs typically cost much more per student than college-preparatory or general programs cost. A fourth factor is that the cities have a relatively high proportion of elementary children enrolled in high-cost compensatory programs. Besides all these cost problems, there is a set of other less visible cost-increasing factors at play: highly transient school enrollment, need for extensive health services in some schools, and so on.

Even though cities may be able to economize on some items, such as pupil transportation, it is only to be expected that costs per pupil will rise in the future. Indeed, if cities provided the educational services their populations appear to need, it is not unlikely that the cost per pupil would approach that sustained by our richer suburbs.

The financial picture of central cities is not yet complete. Generally speaking, large cities have quite large amounts of taxable real property. Assessed valuation per pupil is high. This means that cities receive rather small amounts in state grants for education, because, as we noted in Chapter 4, most education grants are distributed so that the larger sums are paid to places where assessed valuation per pupil is low; the grants are intended to "equalize" local taxable resources. These education grants are by far the largest type of state distribution to localities.

Central cities also incur extraordinary cost because of nonschool municipal services. There are two basic reasons. Because central cities are the haven for the unfortunate of our land, the cities naturally have large obligations to meet for health and welfare services. Second, the cities have extremely large daytime populations for which they must supply fire, police, and street maintenance services. In most cases cities are unable to levy a tax on these daytime populations commensurate with the costs they impose.

In summary, the "financial plight" of the cities is traceable to several conditions: (1) that school costs are relatively high and unyielding, (2) that state grants-in-aid are concentrated in the functional area of education, and (3) that, accordingly, state grants do not take account of the large needs of the cities to spend for public services, most especially in the nonschool (or municipal) service areas.

The central city has problems other than financial, however, and perhaps the chief of these is to obtain effective coordination and joint planning of all the local public services. Whatever the most strident ills of the city are—crime in the streets, functional illiteracy, broken homes, or unemployment—the cures do not rest upon the ministration of any single service. Good schools must be matched by decent housing, by open green spaces, by clean, cheap public transportation, by well-equipped youth centers, libraries, and athletic facilities.

Attempts at coordination are being pushed at forced draft by the federal government. For example, in the implementation of the Area Redevelopment Act, the Manpower Development and Training Act, and the Vocational Education Act of 1963, city school authorities find themselves engaging in cooperative activities with state and federal labor departments, health and welfare departments, and private firms. The Office of Economic Opportunity is seeking to foster programs under which special school programs for use with children from disadvantaged homes are also made available for adult illiterates. Under the Elementary and Secondary Education Act of 1965, local public school authorities are encouraged to develop cooperative programs with the private schools.

These efforts at coordination and planning of local services are now being made in the face of a long tradition of localism and separatism in school government, and this does not help matters. As we have just noted, the definition of a personnel structure in the school services has not been well accomplished. Indeed, the schools generally have lagged behind municipal governments in establishing workable schemes of position classification. In spite of the difficulties, our age in America may be judged in significant measure by whether metropolitan life remains stunted, ugly, and fragmented or whether it is transformed into something worthy of our scientific accomplishments. Cities can be places that nourish the intellect, the senses, and the soul. The quality of education they offer their permanent residents is crucial, and bigness, fortunately, is no enemy of excellence in education, as the examples of London and Toronto show. To create a climate of education to serve the needs of an urban society is the challenge for the teacher of tomorrow.

Suggested Readings

Advisory Commission on Intergovernmental Relations. *Performance of Urban Functions: Local and Areawide.* Washington: the Commission, 1963.

BENSON, CHARLES S. *The Cheerful Prospect.* Boston: Houghton Mifflin, 1965.

CONANT, JAMES B. *Shaping Educational Policy.* New York: McGraw-Hill, 1964.

MASON, WARD S. *The Beginning Teacher.* Washington: Government Printing Office, 1961.

MEYERSON, MARTIN; TERRETT, BARBARA; and WHEATON, WILLIAM L. C. *Housing, People, and Cities.* New York: McGraw-Hill, 1962.

TINBERGEN, JAN. *Economic Policy: Principles and Design.* Amsterdam: North-Holland, 1964.